NATIVE POLICY
IN SOUTHERN AFRICA

NATIVE POLICY
IN SOUTHERN AFRICA

AN OUTLINE

BY

IFOR L. EVANS
Fellow of St John's College
Cambridge

CAMBRIDGE
AT THE UNIVERSITY PRESS
1934

CAMBRIDGE
UNIVERSITY PRESS

32 Avenue of the Americas, New York NY 10013-2473, USA

Cambridge University Press is part of the University of Cambridge.

It furthers the University's mission by disseminating knowledge in the pursuit of education, learning and research at the highest international levels of excellence.

www.cambridge.org
Information on this title: www.cambridge.org/9781107455795

© Cambridge University Press 1934

First published 1934
First paperback edition 2014

A catalogue record for this publication is available from the British Library

ISBN 978-1-107-45579-5 Paperback

PREFACE

AFRICA, South of the Zambezi, offers a marked contrast to what one may call the Tropics proper. It differs, amongst other things, in that it has a relatively large White population, though, even so, the Native population is much larger: and in that this local European minority is, in the main, responsible for the destinies of White and Black alike. The exceptions to these generalizations only serve to intensify the contrast.

For several years the author of this little book has been engaged in studying some of the problems which confront Great Britain in the African Tropics. In 1933 he visited the South for the first time, and was struck, in spite of obvious differences, by the relevance of many issues there to those elsewhere. He could not find, however, a recent summary, in succinct form, of Native policy in the Union and adjacent territories to help him. He therefore had to make one for himself, and this is now offered to others in the hope that it may save them trouble.

The historical side has been reduced to the absolute minimum necessary for an understanding of existing legislation. It has, in any case, received considerable attention from several South African writers. In the following pages an attempt has been made to present a number of connected facts bearing on the present situation in a manner so far as possible impersonal and uncontroversial. The implications inherent in the facts are left, in general, to those better qualified to judge than any passing traveller can ever hope to be.

Southern Africa, for all its problems, is a delightful country and the hospitality of its people is proverbial. Thanks are due to many friends who would doubtless wish to remain anonymous: but, on this side, grateful mention must be made of the patient courtesy of Mr Evans Lewin, M.B.E., Librarian of the Royal Empire Society, and members of his staff.

All notes and references to sources have been collected together in a separate section. The map gives an approximate idea of the geographical distribution of Native areas South of the Zambezi. So far as the Union is concerned, it is based, with kind permission, on an outline map compiled by the South African Institute of Race Relations.

IFOR L. EVANS

June 1934

CONTENTS

PART I

THE UNION OF SOUTH AFRICA

1. *Native policy before the act of union*

WHEN Europeans first settled at the Cape in 1652 they found a country sparsely inhabited by wandering Bushmen and Hottentots. In the process of time, the former were either exterminated or driven away, while the latter were in many cases enslaved or otherwise absorbed. A few still exist in remote areas, and Hottentot blood also survives, with generous admixture, in the people known as the 'Cape Coloured'.

In the early days of the Dutch East India Company, assistance was given to European immigrants, though a few slaves were imported for employment as domestic servants and semi-skilled artisans. Before very long, however, White labour came to be regarded with disfavour. It was expensive and liable to be too independent for the tastes of a bureaucratic administration. The policy of assisted immigration was therefore abandoned, and, during the eighteenth century, fresh supplies of labour were obtained by importing Negro slaves from West Africa and Mozambique, and delinquent Malays from the East Indies. Fortunately plantation slavery never really took root in the Cape. Under British rule, moreover, the Slave Trade was abolished in 1807, while twenty-six years later, an Act of the Imperial Parliament emancipated all the slaves in British Colonies and provided compensation for their former owners. In South Africa the process was complete in 1838, and though the institution of slavery added its quota to the coloured population, it did not survive long enough to influence the evolution of Native policy.

As the frontier of settlement advanced eastwards, White pioneers came into contact with the vanguard of a Bantu migration from the North. These tribes were collectively known as Kaffirs, or unbelievers, a name they had received from the Moslems of the East Coast. They were no more and no less 'native' to South Africa than were the White colonists themselves. When they first appear on the stage of colonial history, what is now called the 'Native problem' was essentially a problem of frontiers.

The dividing line between European and Abantu up to the first half of the nineteenth century lay somewhere between the Great Fish and the Kei Rivers. Government policy aimed at maintaining peace on the frontier, and the establishment, towards the middle of the century, of British Kaffraria —the nucleus of the country conveniently described as the Ciskei—was an attempt to create a buffer between the Colony and the Bantu tribes farther to the East.

With the arrival of Sir George Grey in 1854, a forward policy was vigorously pursued. The new Governor proposed to gain an influence over all the Bantu tribesmen included between the then existing boundary of the Cape of Good Hope and the new Colony of Natal. This led to a series of annexations, which began in 1855, and ended in 1894 with the acquisition of Pondoland. In the process friendly tribes were confirmed in the occupation of land, while rebellion was usually punished by confiscation. Considerable tracts of country, more especially in the Ciskei, were also set aside for European settlement and ownership.

To win the Natives of the Ciskei to 'civilization and Christianity', Grey encouraged the establishment of schools and hospitals, and endeavoured to create for the local Abantu 'institutions of a civil character suited to their present condition'. (1) Chiefs were given fixed stipends instead of the customary Court fees and perquisites, and European Magistrates were appointed to control the districts. The Chief was entitled to be present at all trials, but he was not greatly encouraged to do so and he had, in any case, lost all pecuniary interest in their outcome. In 1866 British Kaffraria became an integral part of the Cape Colony, and thereafter, with but minor exceptions, Colonial Law alone received official recognition, to the exclusion of Native Law and Custom. The process of detribalization was greatly accelerated, as the judicial, and also, in large measure, the administrative functions of the Chief were assumed by the Magistrate.

The annexation of the territory immediately to the East of the Kei River in 1877 is an important landmark, not only in territorial expansion, but also in the history of Native policy. The principle that European Magistrates should gradually replace the Native Chiefs was, it is true, applied here as in the Ciskeian territories, but Native Law and Custom was always to be administered in civil cases. In criminal matters it was replaced, in 1886, by a special Transkeian Penal Code, which applied to Natives and Europeans alike. In contrast to the Colony proper, legislation was enacted by Proclamation of the Governor, and, prior to Union, no Acts of Parliament were enforced unless expressly extended to these territories. The social status of the Paramount Chiefs was recognized by the payment of stipends and by frequent consultation, while minor Chiefs were appointed Government Headmen, and, as such, were still to play an important though somewhat minor rôle in the administrative machine. To maintain closer contact with Native opinion, Captain Matthew Blyth, one of the pioneer administrators of the territory, anticipated, so early as 1882, that 'a sort of Municipal Council be formed in each district'. [2]

In 1894 a ministry presided over by Cecil Rhodes introduced a measure which has always been given great prominence in the annals of Native policy in South Africa. (3) The district of Glen Grey, in the Ciskei, was chosen for a thorough-going experiment in detribalization, based upon a complete change in Native land tenure. The district was surveyed, and the arable separated from the grazing. Pasture land was to remain in common, but the arable was divided into individual holdings, on the principle of 'one man one lot'. For these an annual quit rent was payable to Government. A number of safeguards, such as restrictions on the right to alienate, and the prohibition of mortgages, was introduced to protect the individual holder against the possible consequences of his own folly. The Act also aimed at giving the Natives a share in local government. In each location the plot holders were to elect a Location Board. For the district as a whole, a body called the Glen Grey District Council was set up, composed of six members nominated by the Location Boards and six by the Governor, with the District Magistrate as Chairman. The Council was empowered to levy a local rate, fixed in practice at ten shillings a year, to be expended on such objects as cattle dips, roads, and agricultural improvements. Finally, a labour tax was imposed on all adult male Natives who did not go each year to work outside the district. This clause was a feature of attraction to many supporters of the Act in Parliament, but it aroused great resentment amongst the local Natives and was soon repealed.

The importance of the Glen Grey Act is not to be looked for so much in its operation in the Glen Grey district itself, as in the extension of the Council System, which it officially inaugurated, to other Native areas in South Africa. The principle was actually applied by Proclamation to the four western districts of the Transkei before the Act came into force in Glen Grey, though the scheme very nearly failed at the outset on account of the opposition aroused by the hated Labour Tax. This, however, soon became a dead letter, and was finally abolished in 1905. Moreover, the introduction of compulsory individual quit-rent tenure was not part of the original plan in the Transkei, and even to-day it has only been attempted in seven districts out of twenty-six.

As first established, each District Council in the Transkei was composed of six members, two being Government nominees and four nominated, from among their own number, by a meeting of all the Headmen of the district. Since 1906, however, Council ratepayers, in districts where individual quit-rent tenure has been applied, have selected three representatives from each location who combine to nominate four of their number for Council membership. In every case the District Council is presided over by the local Magistrate.

The most original feature of the scheme was the institution of a 'Transkei General Council', composed of the Chief Magistrate as Chairman, the

Magistrates of the districts concerned, one member appointed by the Governor from each district, and two members nominated by each of the District Councils. The revenue of the General Council was derived primarily from the proceeds of an annual local rate of not less than ten shillings, payable by each adult male, and by each Native woman, widowed or unmarried, occupying a separate portion of land or a hut in a Council area. Expenditure might be incurred, subject to Government sanction, for such purposes as roads, dipping tanks, afforestation and agricultural improvements, including agricultural education.

The object of the Council system was to give the Natives 'a reasonable voice in the management of the internal affairs of the country', [4] and it was extended to other areas East of the Kei as and when the moment seemed opportune. By 1903, Councils were established in thirteen districts, and the central body was re-christened the 'Transkeian Territories General Council'. It discussed general policy and authorized services paid for out of the common treasury. The District Councils, on the other hand, were the executive organs of the General Council, performing a variety of duties on its behalf and also serving as a forum for the expression of local opinion. [5]

In Natal, which was annexed by Great Britain in 1843, Native policy followed a pattern quite differ-

ent from that adopted in the Cape. The early picture
in this eastern colony is completely dominated by
the figure of Theophilus Shepstone, who came as
'Diplomatic Agent to the Native Tribes' in 1845,
and was virtually supreme in his own sphere for the
next thirty years. He was a man of outstanding
personality and greatly respected by the Natives.
At the outset he had to deal with some eighty thousand people who had sought refuge in Natal from
Zulu despotism. These he managed to move into
separate locations without having recourse to the
use of force. Most of the refugees had lost their
Chiefs, but, as no money was available for maintaining a large administrative staff of Europeans,
Shepstone re-established the tribal system. When-
ever possible, scions of former ruling houses were
given jurisdiction: elsewhere the expedient of appointing Government Chiefs had perforce to be
adopted. In 1850 the Lieutenant-Governor was proclaimed Supreme Chief, in place of the former Zulu
King. As a corollary to the system of tribal control,
Native Law and Custom was recognized from the
very beginning, though naturally with certain necessary modifications. Thus witchcraft cases were
frowned upon, while the death penalty was introduced as a punishment for murder. This latter innovation was justified to the Native by the argument
that a man's life belonged to the Supreme Chief, who
would not, in future, be satisfied with compensation
in cattle for property lost through murder. (6)

In order to give the Natives greater security for the lands assigned to them, it was urged that documentary titles should be made over to trustees acting on their behalf. This policy, strongly opposed by the Legislative Council, was adopted in modified form in 1864. All unalienated location land, amounting to over two and a quarter million acres, was accordingly conveyed to the Natal Native Trust, which was, in fact, the Governor and Executive Council acting in this particular capacity. The trustees were to administer the land for the 'support, advantage or well-being' of the Natives concerned. (7) At various times, between 1862 and 1887, land grants were also made to Missionary Societies, to be held by them on behalf of the Natives, but these were finally brought under the conditional control of the Trust in 1903.

Under the Shepstone regime, any appeal from a Magistrate's Court in a Native area, in a case where Natives were concerned, had been heard by the Secretary for Native Affairs—who was none other than Shepstone himself—as representing the Supreme Chief. This exercise of judicial powers by a high administrative official was brought to an end, in 1875, by the creation of the Natal Native High Court, which has exercised criminal jurisdiction over Natives down to the present day. A Commission was appointed at the same time to draw up a Code of Bantu Law, which was promulgated in 1878. Although intended as a guide, and not as in any way

legally binding, its provisions were slavishly adhered
to in actual practice. It was, moreover, supplanted,
in 1891, by a new Code of Native Law which not only
had full binding force, but could only be amended
by Act of Parliament. An element of formal rigidity
was thus introduced into a primitive legal system
essentially fluid in character.

Beyond the North-Eastern frontiers of Natal, the
militant tribalism of the Zulu King maintained a
precarious independence of European control until
the inevitable conflict occurred in 1879—with the
inevitable result. It was not, however, until 1887
that Zululand was actually annexed by the Crown,
and yet another decade was to pass before the territory was incorporated in Natal, which had become
a self-governing colony in 1893. One of the conditions of the transfer was the provision of sufficient
land for Native Reserves. This was finally achieved
in 1909, when a total area of close on four million
acres was vested in the Zululand Native Trust, a
body constituted on lines identical with those of its
prototype in Natal proper. After annexation, the
Governor became the Supreme Chief of Zululand,
and tribalism remained in full vigour. The Natal
Native Code of 1878 was nominally in force, but, in
practice, disputes between Natives were settled
according to local tribal custom.

While the Cape Colony and Natal proceeded on
their several ways, the Boer Republics paid singu-

larly little attention to Native affairs. It must, however, be remembered that the first settlers in the Orange Free State, recognized as an independent entity in 1854, entered a territory which had been largely denuded of its population as a result of internecine tribal wars. Only three small Reserves, with a total area of less than 160,000 acres, were constituted under the Republic, though a steady influx of Natives was taking place from the surrounding territories. The newcomers settled, for the most part, on European farms, and came under the jurisdiction of the ordinary Magistrates. The only innovation of importance after the Boer War was the establishment, in 1907, of Native Reserve Boards, composed of nominated members sitting under a European Chairman, to deal with matters of local interest and empowered to levy a location tax, not exceeding 20s. a year, on each adult male in the Reserve.

Beyond the Vaal River the South African Republic assumed recognizable form towards the middle of the nineteenth century, but the government was weak and the country in a state of virtual anarchy. Native policy existed largely on paper, so far as it can be said to have existed at all. In 1877, however, the territory was annexed by Great Britain, and a special Department of Native Affairs was established. When, as a result of the First Boer

War, independence was regained four years later, a Native Location Commission was set up, in accordance with the terms of the Pretoria Convention. This body was to reserve to the 'Native tribes of the State such locations as they may be fairly and equitably entitled to', (8) and to hold in trust for Natives such land as they themselves might buy. The work actually achieved was useful so far as it went, but a writer, with every sympathy for the Afrikaner point of view, has to confess that 'no Transvaal Government up to the time of Union ever honestly faced the Native land question'. (9) This stricture applies to the British administration after the Second Boer War, though, as a result of the Report of a Commission in 1907, some additions were made to the Reserves then in existence.

The basic statute governing Native Administration in the South African Republic was a Law of 1885 which declared the President of the Republic to be Paramount Chief of the Native population, and accorded him all the power and authority customarily vested in that office. In conjunction with his Executive Council, he could depose Chiefs and appoint others in their place, and such acts were not subject to review by the Judiciary. The 'laws, customs, or usages hitherto existing among the Natives' were to continue in force 'as long as they have not appeared to be in conflict with the general principles of civilization recognised in the civilised world'. (10) Unfortunately, however, the Courts took the view that the Native law relating to marriage was not consistent with civilized principles, and refused to hear cases concerning *lobola*—the cattle which the intended husband agrees to deliver to the parent of his intended wife. This institution of *lobola* is, of course, virtually the basis of tribal life among the Abantu.

District administration was entrusted to the ordinary Magistrate (*Landdrost*), though, where local conditions demanded it, special provision might be made for work connected with Natives. After annexation by the British, the Governor became Paramount Chief, in the Transvaal as in the Orange River Colony, but, apart from abolishing the judicial powers of the Executive over Natives, matters were allowed to remain very much as they were before.

Each of the four Provinces which, on May 31st, 1910, united to form the Union of South Africa had thus evolved an outlook characteristically its own. In the Cape Province proper, the specific institutions and laws of the Natives had been set aside as unworthy of a civilized community, while the ultimate goal held out to the Black man was that he should become as much like the White man as possible. Under the Cape of Good Hope Constitution Ordinance of 1852, and later Colonial Acts, certain qualifications were laid down for the exercise of the Parliamentary vote, but race and colour were not of their number. Thus emerged, by implication, the Cape Native Franchise, which is still exercised by some 12,000 Black voters, (11) and an ideal, expressed later by Cecil Rhodes as 'equal rights for all civilized men South of the Zambezi'. In the Transkeian Territories this policy of assimilation was applied with notable modifications. Native Law and Custom was administered by European officials; the judicial functions of the Chiefs were quietly ignored, though they still had a subordinate political rôle to perform; and advisory Councils were constituted, on a basis partly authoritarian, partly elective. In Natal the object of official policy was 'to maintain and strengthen the tribal system in the interests of the Colony'. (12) In actual working, Native organization was, in large measure, stabilized and stereotyped at the stage it happened to have reached at the advent of the British. The Transvaal officially recognized, but virtually ignored, Native society, and, in any case, provided no geographical setting adequate for its existence, still less for its natural development; while the Free State can hardly be said to have had a Native policy at all.

2. *The administration*

Variations in local practice have very largely persisted down to the present day, for the laws of the four Colonies continued in force after Union, unless repealed or amended by Parliament. In 1910, however, the Governor-General-in-Council assumed all the powers previously exercised by the various Colonial Governors where Natives and Native Lands were concerned. He is Supreme Chief in Natal, the Transvaal and the Free State, though no attempt has been made to extend the principle of paramountcy to the Cape Province where, as we have seen, Native policy had developed on anti-tribal lines. A Native Affairs Department of the Union was established, under the authority of the South Africa Act of 1909, to administer matters hitherto vested in the Native Affairs Departments of the four Colonies. Native affairs as such are thus the direct concern of the Union as a whole, and no longer of the several Provinces.

It would be instructive to follow the discussions which take place periodically on the Native question. We must, however, be content to summarize the concrete results achieved since 1910. As the framing of policy is a paramount consideration, it will be convenient to begin with the Native Affairs Act of 1920, which set up an advisory body, called the Native Affairs Commission, consisting of the Minister of Native Affairs, as Chairman, and not less than three nor more than five other members. These gentlemen are appointed by Government, and receive a salary, but they have no legal security for their tenure of office. They may consider 'any matter relating to the general conduct of the administration of Native affairs, or to legislation in so far as it may affect the Native population', and submit recommendations thereon to the Minister. (13) If their recommendations are not accepted, they may ultimately require that all relative papers be laid before Parliament. In certain matters, more especially those relating to the establishment and constitution of Native Councils, the Minister must seek their advice. They may also recommend that representative Native Conferences be summoned 'with a view to the ascertainment of the sentiments of the Native population...in regard to any measure in so far as it may affect such population'. (14)

When the Commission began to function in 1921, it declared that it was 'primarily and essentially the friend of the Native people', as well as being 'the adviser of the Government where the interests of the Natives are concerned'. As such, it 'should endeavour to win the confidence of the Natives' and also 'to educate public opinion, both Native and non-Native, so as to bring about the most harmonious relations possible between White and Black in South Africa'. (15) This is certainly a very noble aim, but the Commission, as hitherto constituted, contains no Native member and is not usually regarded as sufficiently representative. Its dependent status is a definite hindrance, though it has to its credit much excellent work, more especially of detailed investigation and enquiry. A few Native Conferences have already been summoned upon its recommendation, but it is perhaps too early to attempt

an estimate of this particular departure in the policy
of consultation.

   The organization of district administration—in
many ways the basic problem of government where
Natives are concerned—is greatly complicated, in
South Africa, by the existence, in most areas, of
White and Black side by side. For Europeans, the
requisite instrument is the Magistrate, who is an
official of the Department of Justice. For Natives,
on the other hand, it is obviously desirable to have
men with special knowledge of their Law and
Custom, and a sympathetic understanding of their
general outlook on life. Such experts should clearly
be officers of the Department of Native Affairs. In
1910, however, the local official, in the vast majority
of districts outside the Transkeian Territories, was
a member of the Department of Justice. This naturally had the effect of relegating the Department of
Native Affairs to a secondary place, and made for
interdepartmental friction. Moreover, with the exception once again of the Transkeian Territories, no
organization existed for the local co-ordination of
administrative practice in any of the principal Native
areas of the Union. This deficiency was in part made
good, so far as Natal was concerned, by the appointment of a Chief Native Commissioner for Natal and
Zululand in 1912, (16) a precedent followed in the
Ciskeian Districts eleven years later. In course of

time, moreover, an understanding was reached that the appointment, by the Department of Justice, of Magistrates to districts with a large Native population, would only be made after prior consultation with the Department of Native Affairs.

A most important step towards departmental and interdepartmental co-ordination was the passing of the Native Administration Act in 1927. Amongst many other things, this measure empowered the Governor-General to appoint a Chief Native Commissioner for any area. Up to the present, five high officials of the Department of Native Affairs have been appointed to these posts. They act as local representatives of the Department, and exercise general supervision in all matters where the interests of the Natives and the policy of the Government in Native Affairs are concerned. (17)

Greater co-ordination between the Departments has been achieved by the extension of the device of dual appointment. In predominantly Native areas, Native Commissioners, who are primarily members of the Department of Native Affairs, are also appointed by the Department of Justice to perform the duties of a Magistrate. Similarly, in mixed areas, Magistrates, who are officials of the Department of Justice, are appointed to act as Native Commissioners by the Department of Native Affairs. In this latter case, Additional and Assistant Native Commissioners may also be appointed to meet the special needs of the local Native population. (18)

These provisions have certainly done much to clear the administrative air, but the greater prestige enjoyed in the popular mind by the Department of Justice is reflected in many ways to the detriment of officials of the Department of Native Affairs. This is most unfortunate, for this Department is second to none in importance, if not, indeed, the most vital branch of the public service. (19)

In the administration of Native peoples, specialized experience and individual initiative must necessarily count for much, since conditions vary greatly from one district to the next, and the unexpected may reasonably be expected to happen at any time. It follows that the Executive should have wider discretionary powers than the theory, if not the practice, of modern state life in most communities of the Western European type would allow. Parliament is hardly the proper forum, therefore, for the detailed consideration of Native problems: its procedure is necessarily cumbersome, and the exigencies of party politics not infrequently take precedence over all other considerations. Nevertheless, executive acts must clearly be subject to the possibility of review at any time, and Parliament cannot divest itself of the right, and, indeed, the duty, of determining the broad lines of policy in Native affairs, as in all other matters of import to the State.

The only Native area in the former Colonies in respect of which a working compromise between these conflicting principles had been achieved was the Transkei, where the device of legislation by Proclamation was an essential feature of the administrative scheme. It was extended to all Native areas by the Native Administration Act of 1927, which empowered the Governor-General to repeal or amend any law, or to make new laws, for these areas, by Proclamation in the Gazette. Safeguards against abuse of this power are provided by conditions as to prior publication; by the stipulation that the Proclamation must be presented to Parliament, which may request its repeal or modification; and by the right granted to the Native Affairs Commission of recording dissent from any of its provisions. [20]   A number of Proclamations has already been promulgated, and the variety of topics with which they deal and of districts to which they apply illustrates the practical utility of a mode of procedure so flexible as this. [21]

3. *The land question*

The term 'Native areas' requires careful consideration, since it raises the whole issue of the occupation of land. The historical side of this question has already been briefly touched upon. Europeans had settled in areas where the Abantu had not penetrated, or where they were not permanently established, but they had also occupied a great deal of land elsewhere, regardless of any claims the Natives might have had upon it. (22) But for the intervention of the Imperial Government, the Reserves would have been smaller still.

The statistical position at the time of Union is roughly indicated in the following summary. (23)

	Area (thousand sq. miles)	Population in 1911 (thousands)		Native Reserves (million acres)
		European	Bantu	
Cape	277	582	1520	12·7
Natal	35	98	953	6·3
Transvaal	110	421	1220	1·9
Free State	50	175	326	0·2
Total	472	1276	4019	21·1

It will be seen that the area reserved for Native occupation only amounted to 21 million acres, while the total area of the Union is something over 300 million acres. Allowance must, of course, be made for mountain peaks and semi-desert, which are vested for the most part in the Crown. It must also be borne in mind that certain of the Reserves, such as the Transkei, include some of the best land in the Union, while there are vast areas in European occupation, like the Karroo, which are quite unsuited for any form of intensive agriculture. When all is said, however, this land settlement, most obviously inadequate in the territory of the former Republics, can nowhere be described as erring on the side of generosity to the Natives.

For many years prior to Union, economic and other pressure had led to a great increase in the number of Natives living outside the Reserves, and 'Land Hunger' had become as characteristic a feature of the Abantu as of most other peasants throughout the World. In the Cape Province, and, with relatively minor exceptions, in Natal, there were no legal restrictions to prevent Natives from acquiring land. In the Transvaal they enjoyed the same right under the Pretoria Convention of 1881, though it was long the practice that any land they purchased should be held in trust on their behalf. A decision of the Supreme Court in 1905, however, recognized their claim to hold land in their own names. (24) On the other hand, in the Free State, with one small exception, Natives were prevented by law from purchasing any land whatsoever. In three out of the four Provinces, therefore, the acquisition by Natives of land outside the Reserves was limited by their ability to pay for it, rather than by any legal restrictions. In the Transvaal and the Cape a considerable area was actually acquired, sometimes by individuals, but more frequently by tribes or syndicates of Natives.

These purchases were on too small a scale to satisfy the aspirations of an ever-increasing mass of landless persons, some of whom drifted into the towns, while more squatted on land not specially reserved for their use. In spite of earlier prohibitions, a large number settled on Crown Land, more particularly in the Transvaal and Natal. Their position was to some extent recognized in that they were called upon in due course to pay an annual rent. This was fixed in 1903 at 40s. for each hut in Natal, and at 20s., increased twenty years later to 30s., for each adult male in the Transvaal. The squatters have no security of tenure and may be called upon to leave their holdings at short notice. The amount of Crown Land at present occupied under this rather unsatisfactory system has been estimated at something under 1¾ million acres in Natal, and at well over 3 million acres in the Transvaal. (25) The numbers involved are relatively very small in the Cape Province, while no Native is allowed to reside on Government land in any district in the Free State without the written permission of the Magistrate.

Squatting on Crown Land certainly eased the pressure in some areas, but its possibilities were strictly limited. An ever-increasing flow of Native labour was thus of necessity directed to private land in European ownership. If Natives were taken on as farm hands, they were paid a monthly wage, which was usually supplemented by the right to cultivate a small plot of land and to graze a limited number of stock on the farm. The farmer, however, was frequently able to obtain as much labour as he wanted without paying any money wage at all. He merely allowed Natives to settle on his farm, giving them land to cultivate and grazing for their cattle, while they performed certain stipulated labour services in return. These varied, in different districts, from sixty to one hundred and eighty days annually, the most usual being work by the man and his family for ninety days, distributed throughout the agricultural year. Some farmers found it more profitable to work less of their land themselves and to allow Natives to reside, cultivate and keep cattle on their farms in return for a share, usually one half, of the crops they harvested. This produce-sharing tenancy, or 'ploughing on halves', as it is sometimes called, was particularly prevalent in the Free State. In the Northern Transvaal, where large blocks of land are owned by investment companies, it was, and still is, more common to find informal agreements under which Natives occupy land in return for an annual money rental, with grazing fees payable in addition. Finally, there were a few cases of ordinary leasehold tenure in various parts of the Cape, Natal and the Transvaal.

The unsatisfactory nature of much of this development had become apparent for many years before Union. Labour tenancy is distinctly inefficient, and is often productive of friction between farmers and Natives. (26) Produce-sharing tenancy and various forms of leasehold have encountered even more criticism. The former is in many ways uneconomic, while both make for landlordism, an institution out of harmony with the aspirations of all who believe in the future of European farming in

South Africa. It is not surprising, therefore, to find
that these matters should have been the subject of
legislation in the several Colonies. In the Cape Province, no 'private location' could be established on
any property without a licence, renewable annually,
and the payment of a fee in respect of each Native
tenant. (27) In the Transvaal, not more than five
Native households were allowed to reside on any
single property owned by a European without official
permission, though the effect of this restriction was
very largely nullified in that any White tenant, or
'bywoner', living on a farm had also the right to
keep five Native families, subject only to the permission of the landowner. (28) Natal legislation was
honoured in the breach rather than the observance,
but in the Free State the limitation to five of the
number of Native families who might reside on any
one farm was more carefully defined and more
strictly enforced than elsewhere. (29)

The situation thus briefly outlined was subjected
to close scrutiny by an Inter-Colonial Commission
soon after the Boer War. The whole future relationship between White and Black in South Africa was
clearly involved in this all-important question of the
land. Representative European opinion already in-
clined to the view that, so far, at least, as the possession of land was concerned, the separation of European and Abantu on a territorial basis would be in
the best interests of both races. The creation of
Native Reserves had been a first step in this direc-

tion, but insufficient land had been provided to meet the needs of a stationary, still more of an expanding population. On the other hand, the uncontrolled flow of Native labour to European farms led inevitably to the manifold evils of the squatter system, which should, it was argued, be made subject to Government control and the payment of an annual licence fee. On the broader question of principle, a majority of the Commission recommended that the purchase of land by Natives 'should in future be limited to certain areas to be defined by legislative enactment'. (30)

Partial effect was given to these views by the Natives Land Act of 1913, which was intended to be a temporary measure, but has actually remained in force down to the present day. Its principal object was to maintain the then existing balance in the occupation and ownership of land, as between Europeans and Natives, until a final delimitation could be arrived at on the basis of the recommendations of a Commission to be set up under the Act. Meanwhile certain lands, which included the Native Reserves then in existence, together with farms held in trust for Natives in the Transvaal, were defined as 'scheduled areas', outside which no Native might purchase or hire land from any person other than a Native without the approval of the Governor-General. On the other hand, no person other than a Native might purchase or hire land either in a scheduled area, or from a Native outside a scheduled area, save with the same official approval. It was laid down, however, that nothing in the Act which might have the effect of preventing a person from obtaining the necessary qualifications for registration as a Parliamentary voter should be in force in the Cape. This was later held, by the Supreme Court, to mean that the restrictions on the purchase and hire of land were inoperative in that Province. (31) The Cape Province, moreover, was not affected by the special provisions against squatting contained in the Act. In the Free State, on the other hand, it was made illegal for Natives to hold land on a produce-sharing basis, but in Natal and the Transvaal, a Native already registered for taxation purposes on a particular farm, might continue under this system, until ejected by the owner. In all three Provinces, however, the squatter was ultimately to give place to the farm labourer, by which is meant a Native who, in consideration of his being allowed to reside upon a farm, renders the owner at least ninety days' service in the calendar year, but pays no rent and gives no valuable consideration of any kind other than service. (32) It will be seen that this definition covers both the farm hand in receipt of a money wage, and the Native who holds land under a labour tenancy. As it was one of the principal objects of these provisions to assure a plentiful supply of labour, the statutory limitation on the number of Natives allowed to reside as farm labourers on any one farm in the Transvaal was repealed. (33)

To make effective the particular form of what has been called 'possessory segregation' embodied in the Natives Land Act of 1913, it was essential to decide, once and for all, what areas should be set apart within which Natives and Europeans respectively should be debarred from acquiring or hiring land or interests in land. The necessary enquiry was undertaken by a Commission which sat under the chairmanship of Sir William Beaumont, and finally issued its report in 1916. In the ensuing discussions there was general agreement as to the inadequacy of the 'scheduled areas', but the schedule of additional Native areas recommended by the Commission met with considerable opposition in detail. The proposals were therefore referred to five Local Committees, specially appointed for the purpose. These reported in their turn in 1918, but their recommendations, which were, on the whole, less favourable to Native claims, proved no more acceptable than those of the Beaumont Commission. The solution of such a problem on parliamentary lines is indeed immensely difficult of achievement. A multitude of local interests is involved, and any attempt to apply a uniform scheme to all four Provinces is almost bound to raise the question of the Native Franchise in the Cape. The issue, shelved in 1920, was taken up anew by General Hertzog six years later as part of a comprehensive programme touching almost every aspect of Native policy in the Union. His Natives Land (Amendment) Bill was introduced in 1929, but it was not proceeded with, since the real test measure—the Natives Parliamentary Representation Bill—failed to obtain the requisite majority. (34) The Act of 1913, therefore, still holds the field.

While this much abused measure prohibited the purchase of land by a Native from a non-Native outside the scheduled areas, it fortunately left a loophole in the phrase 'except with the approval of the Governor-General'. This was originally intended to meet individual cases of hardship, but, with the patent failure of Parliament to provide a solution, it enabled the legislative deficiency to be made good, in part at least, by executive action. Thus in 1918 it was agreed to recommend, for the Governor-General's approval, genuine applications on the part of Natives for the purchase or lease of land in any area recommended for Native occupation both by the Beaumont Commission and by a Local Committee. This was changed, in 1922, to any area approved by a Local Committee, while the present basis of recommendation is the schedule of released areas contained in the Natives Land (Amendment) Bill of 1929, which embodies the proposals of the Local Committees in somewhat modified form. (35) Several thousand applications have actually been granted in this way, and some financial assistance has also been provided for the purchase, in such areas, of land for occupation by landless Natives. Meanwhile, however, the future of the rural population still remains, to-day as at the time of Union, the most important issue in the Native life of South Africa.

4. *Natives in urban areas*

More spectacular, perhaps, than the land question, is the complex of problems raised by the steadily increasing flow of Natives to urban areas. The people concerned are of two main types. Some are inhabitants of the Reserves who need money to pay their taxes, and to satisfy new desires by the purchase of commodities which a primitive subsistence economy cannot provide. They come periodically to work in the mines, and also, to some extent, in other industrial undertakings. Others are Natives, for whom no adequate supply of land is usually available in the Reserves, who settle in or near the towns. While the former maintain close contact with their home districts, to which they almost invariably return at the end of each period of work, the latter tend to become permanently urbanized.

The position of Natives employed or recruited for employment upon mines and works is governed by the Native Labour Regulation Act of 1911. This measure amended and consolidated earlier colonial legislation, and established unity in administrative practice by the appointment of a Director of Native Labour for the Union. It was made compulsory for

all labour agents and compound managers to obtain
a licence each year from the Director, who thus
exercises control over recruiting and general organization. He is assisted in this task by a staff of In-
spectors, who have summary jurisdiction in the case
of minor offences committed by Native labourers,
and power to enquire into any grievances which may
arise. The Act simplified control over recruiting by
insisting upon a written contract, attested before
a Magistrate or some other recognized person, for
each Native recruited by a labour agent. Closer
control over conditions of labour was facilitated by
the power to proclaim as 'Labour Districts' areas
where large numbers of Natives are employed in
mining or industrial concerns. In such districts,
stricter regulations are in force, and any employer
providing accommodation for fifty Native labourers
or more must appoint a compound manager,
licensed by the Director, to supervise and control
them. The Act also regulated the payment of compensation to Native labourers in cases of incapacita-
tion or death arising out of their employment. (36)

An important feature of this measure was the
power conferred upon the Governor-General to issue
Regulations governing the application in detail of
the general principles it enunciated. Regulations
have, in fact, been framed to deal with almost every
conceivable aspect of the problem. In particular,
they lay down certain minimum standards in matters
such as accommodation, food, and hospital services,

and provide for the medical examination of every Native prior to his employment in any mine or industrial undertaking within the scope of the Act. The power to regulate the granting of advances, in cash or in kind, as an inducement to Natives to enter into contracts of employment, was extended, in 1921, to cover every class of agent and employment, (37) and the Regulations now in force reduce the dangers of this particular form of pressure to a minimum.

It is only fair to add that the great improvement which has taken place during the last twenty years in the general position of Natives working on the gold mines of the Witwatersrand—which dominate the Native labour situation as they do every other aspect of economic life in South Africa—is to be attributed at least as much to the policy adopted by the industry itself as to any measure of government control. Under the aegis of the Chamber of Mines, a powerful body representative of all the groups operating on the Rand, a most efficient organization has been built up to deal with the recruiting of Native labour. (38) Many of the workers come to the mines on their own initiative; others, known as Assisted Voluntary Workers, obtain advances in their home districts to cover such items as the railway fare to Johannesburg; while less than half now engage for work through labour agents. In the encouragement of thrift, by the system of voluntary deferred pay, introduced in 1918; in the activities of its Accidents Committee, which does everything humanly possible to diminish the risks attendant upon mining operations; and in many other ways besides, the Chamber of Mines works in close collaboration with the various Government Departments concerned. Of course the temporary segregation of thousands of adult male Natives in large compounds is an unnatural system, even though it unfortunately appears to be inevitable under the circumstances prevailing on the Rand. Within the limits of the possible, however, very much is done to make the workers cheerful and contented. As regards housing, food, and living conditions generally, the standard observed in the vast majority of the compounds is far in advance of the minimum required by Government Regulations. The provision of social amenities is actively encouraged by the Chamber of Mines, and compound management has become a fine art. The motive of this admirable administrative organization may well be self-interest, but it is none the less enlightened on that account.

In comparison with the situation prevailing in most mine compounds, the living conditions of the majority of urban Natives were, and, though to a decreasing extent, still are extremely bad. In colonial days responsibility for these people lay with the local authorities in whose areas they happened to reside. It was usual for them to be segregated in special locations, but the statutory powers conferred upon the local authorities were inadequate, and public opinion was not as yet alive to the importance of the issues involved. The prevalence of disease in many of these slums, and the danger of the spread of infection to adjacent European areas gradually became apparent, more especially during the influenza epidemic of 1918, while the rapid growth of the Native urban population made the problem a pressing one. In 1923, therefore, the Natives (Urban Areas) Act was passed to provide, amongst other things, for improved conditions of residence for Natives and for the better administration of Native Affairs in or near urban areas.

The responsibility of the local authorities is maintained under the Act. They are given the power, subject, in each case, to the approval of the Minister for Native Affairs, to remove or abolish existing locations; to set up new locations; to provide hostels and dwellings, or to assist Natives to build their own houses, in the locations; and to borrow the money necessary for these purposes. If any local authority should appear to have neglected its duties under the Act, the Minister may order a public enquiry to be held. If the evidence warrant it, he may then require that proper provision be made for the Natives concerned, and, in the last resort, he may even give instructions for the necessary works to be carried out at the expense of the local authority in question.

The Act also facilitates the application, in all

urban areas, of the principle of compulsory residential segregation, which was already provided for by earlier legislation in the Transvaal and the Free State. It empowers the Governor-General, by Proclamation, to enforce the residence in a location of Natives living within the limits of any urban area. (39) Such action is not taken, in actual practice, unless adequate accommodation is available, and certain classes of Natives, notably domestic servants, are in any case exempt. The operation of the general principle of segregation is made more effective by the stipulation that, with certain specified exceptions, no Natives may settle within three miles of an urban boundary.

If Natives are to be excluded from European areas, it is only natural that Europeans should be prohibited from acquiring land or premises in the locations, and that trading sites should be reserved for Natives, or for the local authority itself. Moreover, all revenue collected in a location must be paid into a special Native Revenue Account, the proceeds being earmarked for expenditure for location purposes, under the general supervision of the Department of Native Affairs. The management of each location is, of course, vested in the local authority, which appoints one or more Location Superintendents, licensed by the Minister. A Native Advisory Board, composed of not less than three Native members, and a Chairman, who may be a European, must, however, be consulted as to any regulation which the local authority may propose to make for the location. The Act thus applies, in the case of urban Natives, the principle of consultation, which is the essential feature of the Council system as it exists amongst the rural population of the Reserves.

Conditions of living in urban areas have certainly shown marked signs of improvement since 1923. Local authorities have been stimulated into action, and some of the leading municipalities have embarked upon a large-scale programme of slum clearance. Financial support has taken two principal forms, both of which were contemplated in the Act. In Johannesburg, houses in the new locations are provided, in the main, by the Municipality, and rented to the Natives. It is interesting to notice, incidentally, that as this is a municipal enterprise, building operations are performed by White labour. This results in higher costs, and therefore higher rentals, than would be necessary if Native labour were employed. In Bloemfontein, where the alternative method is in force, financial assistance is given to Natives to enable them to build their own houses in the location. One or other of these systems has been followed in a large number of towns in the Union, but while much has been accomplished, more remains to be done, and the number of Natives in urban areas is still increasing.

The Act of 1923 aimed not only at improving conditions in urban areas: it also provided machinery designed to control the influx of Natives to the towns. With this end in view, it gave power to the Governor-General to proclaim areas in which every male Native, with certain specified exceptions, must carry either a permit to seek work, or a duly registered service contract. If he fail to find work within a given period of time, he may be compelled to leave the proclaimed area. The Governor-General was also empowered to prohibit altogether the entry of Natives, for the purpose of residence or employment, into any specified urban area, save under conditions specially proclaimed. This very drastic measure of control can be introduced on the application of the local authority responsible for the area in question, but the procedure has only been followed as yet in a very small number of cases.

The enforcement of the carrying of permits or registered service contracts in proclaimed areas is, of course, one particular aspect of the Pass System, which had long been applied, in one form or another, in all the Territories, with the exception of the Cape Province proper, where Vagrancy Laws were in force. The system is defended on the ground that it affords protection to honest Natives; that it is necessary for purposes of identification and the prevention of crime; that it is of great assistance in the enforcement of contractual obligations; and that it succeeds in checking the wholesale entry of Natives into towns. It is bitterly resented by many Natives by reason of the drastic restrictions it imposes on the liberty of movement of the individual, and, probably even more, on account of the manner in which it is only too frequently applied by subordinate officials. The Native Economic Commission of 1930–2 reported that there could be no question that the pass requirements of the northern Provinces were onerous upon the Native people, and that an undesirable effect of their enforcement was the creation of a large volume of technically criminal offences, which involve little or no moral opprobrium. (40).

There may be two opinions as to the practical merits of this particular attempt at solving what is, after all, a very real problem, but it would probably be generally agreed that, if it is to be maintained at all, 'some simplification of the existing pass system is overdue'. (41) This could, in fact, be achieved by executive action, for wide powers were conferred upon the Governor-General, by the Native Administration Act of 1927, to deal with the whole question by Proclamation. It is important to note, however, that no Native area, as scheduled in the Natives Land Act of 1913 or any amending Act, may be included within a pass area. (42) In specially proclaimed urban areas, on the other hand, curfew regulations are also in force. (43)

A feature of the system is the fact that Coloured persons are specifically excluded from its operation. (44) If the prevention of crime be a major object, this distinction is hard to justify, for the proportion of criminal convictions, other than those

under the Pass Laws themselves, is higher amongst
the Coloured population than amongst the Natives.

5. *Taxation and development*

The principle of racial differentiation extends to the
important field of taxation. In the case of Europeans and Coloured persons, direct taxation in the
Union is based on the principle of ability to pay: in
the case of Natives it takes the more primitive form
of a fixed sum payable each year. In early colonial
days every effort had been made to ensure that the
Native territories should be self-supporting, and a
hut tax was levied upon the tribesmen with this end
in view. The amount was finally fixed at 14*s.* a year
in Natal, and at 10*s.* in the Cape, though Natives
holding land on individual tenure paid their annual
quit rent instead. In the case of those living in
Council Districts, such as Glen Grey or the Transkei,
a personal tax of 10*s.* a year for local purposes was
imposed in addition. The other Colonies adopted the
principle of a poll tax, fixed at 20*s.* in the Free State,
where residents of Native Reserve Board areas also
paid a local tax of 20*s.*; and at 40*s.* in the Transvaal,
where half the amount was, however, remitted to
residents in urban locations and to farm labourers.
This somewhat anomalous situation was allowed to
continue for many years after Union, and it was not
until the passing of the Natives Taxation and Development Act, in 1925, that the various systems

were co-ordinated. A general poll tax of 20s., payable annually by all adult males, was then instituted throughout the Union, together with a local tax of 10s., payable by the occupiers of every hut or dwelling in the Reserves and in certain other specified areas. This local tax is not, and cannot be, applied under the Act to the inhabitants of urban locations controlled by a local authority. (45) It is essentially a tax upon Native landholders.

The reform of the system of direct taxation introduced in 1925 was very closely bound up with the question of expenditure on Native services, and, more especially, on Native education. The earliest attempts to provide schools for Native children had been made by pioneer evangelists in the early part of the nineteenth century. For the first fifty years, such educational facilities as existed were financed and managed entirely by missionary societies. The various Governments then gave some measure of financial assistance, which increased steadily as the years went by. With it there grew up a system of Government control, exercised in all four Colonies through the Minister of Education, and not through the Department of Native Affairs. The South Africa Act made primary and secondary education the concern of the various Provinces, (46) and as almost all Native education was and is of this character, it has remained under Provincial control.

The revenue of the Provinces is, of course, derived very largely from subsidies received from the Union Government. Down to 1922, no part of these subsidies had been specially earmarked for Native education, but, in the financial year 1921–2, the following sums were actually expended on this service by the various Provinces: (47)

Cape Province	£240,000
Natal	49,000
Transvaal	46,000
Orange Free State	5,000
Total	£340,000

On the plea that Native education was becoming too costly, the Transvaal Government proposed to levy an additional tax on Natives in 1921. This brought matters to a head, and led, in the following year, to legislation prohibiting the Provincial Councils from imposing any direct taxation upon Natives, and requiring them to spend each year on Native education a sum not less, or not less in proportion to their total education vote, than that actually spent in the financial year 1921–2. It also empowered the Governor-General to make grants for the improvement of Native education in any Province out of revenue derived from the direct taxation of Natives. (48)

This was the situation which the Natives Taxation and Development Act was designed to meet. Native taxation was co-ordinated throughout the several Provinces with a view to increasing its total yield. One-fifth of the proceeds of the general tax, together with the local tax and Native quit rents, was to be paid into a fund called the Native Development Account. As from the financial year 1926–7, this Account has received, in addition, an annual contribution from Union Funds amounting to £340,000, which was the amount spent by the various Provinces upon Native education in the year 1921–2. (49) Thereafter the Provincial Councils were relieved of their obligation to earmark a definite sum for that particular purpose.

The revenue of the Native Development Account is to be expended, after consultation with the Native Affairs Commission, primarily 'for the maintenance, extension and improvement of educational facilities amongst Natives', and 'for the further development and the advancement of the welfare of Natives'. (50)

For the six years 1926–7 to 1931–2, the share of the general tax paid into the Account has averaged some £240,000 which, together with the grant from the Union Government of £340,000, makes a total of approximately £580,000 a year. Annual grants from the Account to the Provincial administrations, for the purposes of Native Education, have averaged about £530,000 a year, and constitute the principal charge upon general revenue. Something has also been done for agricultural development. Thus a Native Agricultural School was opened at Fort Cox in the Ciskei, and a considerable number of its students are already employed as Agricultural Demonstrators in various Native areas.

The local revenue of the Account—derived from the local tax and quit-rent payments—has averaged a little over £250,000 a year during the same period. This money is expended within the prescribed areas in which it is collected. Approximately two-thirds of the total is handed over to the various local Councils and Boards, while most of the balance is devoted to the dipping of stock owned by Natives outside the Council Districts.

The Native Development Account has also had to provide for the repayment of advances made in earlier years by the Union Government to the various Provincial Councils for the augmentation of the salaries of Native teachers. This involved a total burden of approximately £220,000, spread over a period of eight years. (51)

The institution of the Native Development Account has certainly given an impetus to the provision of Native services. Its existence is largely responsible for the increase in the total sum spent by Government on Native education from £340,000 in 1921–2 to over £600,000 ten years later, and for additional expenditure on agricultural development. As its revenue, however, consists of a fixed annual grant, together with a percentage of the proceeds of one relatively rigid form of taxation, it is very inelastic. One is thus faced with the anomaly that the development of Native services has to be financed by a fund which is itself almost incapable of development.

Underlying all this legislation, moreover, is a principle of the very first importance. Prior to 1922, Government assistance to Native education may have been inadequate, but it was nevertheless recognized, by implication at least, as a national obligation, and was financed out of general revenue. Since that date any expansion in the admittedly limited facilities then in existence must, in effect, be paid for out of revenue derived from Native sources, or else by private charity. Native education has thus come to be regarded as a Native rather than a national service, and the advancement of the poorest section of the population is made dependent upon its own very limited resources. This principle is not applied in the case of the Asiatic and Coloured inhabitants of the Union, for whom educational grants are made by Government on a *per caput* basis. It may be irrelevant, though not, perhaps, without interest, to add that, with the relatively rare exception of such as are assessable for Income Tax, these people, together with a large proportion of the Whites, pay no direct taxation whatsoever.

The policy of regarding the Natives as an entirely separate community, financing its own services out of its own resources, might not lead to any serious difficulty in actual practice if complete residential segregation existed on a territorial basis. As this is not and cannot be the case, it is obviously extremely difficult to assess the proportion of total revenue contributed by the Native population, and the proportion of total expenditure reasonably chargeable to them. This was, however, one of the terms of reference of the Native Economic Commission of 1930–2.

In considering the total revenue of the State, the Commission made allocations on the basis of the estimated amount paid, directly or indirectly, by Natives. This was a simple matter so far as specifically Native taxes were concerned. It became more complicated when receipts from Customs and Excise were analysed, though some commodities are known to be imported wholly or predominantly for Native consumption, while others are hardly consumed at all by Natives. It became purely arbitrary when such items as mining revenue were under consideration. As the amount directly paid by Natives in Income Tax and Death Duties is negligible, these were left out of account altogether.

On the expenditure side, the specifically Native services presented no difficulty. For certain joint services, like police and prisons, the number of offences and convictions offered some rough guide. For the rest, with modifications here and there where evidence was available, the proportion chargeable to the Native population was taken as approximately one-eighth, which is their estimated share of the total National Income of the country. The same ratio was also adopted, on the revenue side, in the

case of the 'Public Estate', which includes mining
revenues other than Income Tax, rents of Government Property, and the like. The final result of a
great deal of detailed investigation on these lines
gave the following figures for the financial year
1929–30: (52)

	Million £	
	Revenue	Expenditure
Total, Union and Provinces	35·7	35·8
Estimated Native Share	3·3	4·2

These figures taken by themselves prove very little,
unless it be the enormous difference in economic development between the Natives and the rest of the
community. Detailed analysis might suggest points
of criticism here and there. Thus one member of the
Commission would add half a million, under the
head of the 'Public Estate', to the Revenue allocated to Natives by the rest of his colleagues. It has
been suggested, moreover, that the Native share of
police and prisons is bound to be high, because there
are many offences, such as being without a pass, or
failing to pay poll tax, that they alone can commit,
but which are not considered as crimes in most
parts of the world. From yet another angle it might
be argued that the existing form of administration
in Native areas is unnecessarily expensive, and that
considerable economies might be effected if more
use were made of Native agencies. These and similar

arguments are, however, no criticism of the work of the Commission, which is here concerned with the machinery of government as it is and not as it might be. The real criticism should rather be of the standpoint which prompted this particular enquiry for, as the Commissioners themselves observe, 'it is not usual in treatises on Public Finance to consider taxation and public expenditure from the point of view of any one class of persons'. (53)

It may be possible to make a rough estimate of the share of the National Income at present received by Natives. It is infinitely more difficult to assess the importance of their contribution to that National Income. The gold mining industry, upon which the prosperity of South Africa and the Revenue of the Union Government so largely depend, is the result of European capital and organization working with Native labour. It is a joint enterprise, and its success demands the continued collaboration of all parties concerned. The problem of the further development of the Native peoples, whether in the mines, the cities or the fields, must indeed be viewed in relation to the contribution they can make, both as producers and consumers, to the economic life of the country as a whole. There is no obvious reason why it should be associated with a percentage of the yield of a particular tax.

6. *Administration of justice*

Native advancement is not merely a question of formal education, nor even of improved agricultural methods, vital though these may be. It also involves the association of the governed in the work of government, with a view to helping them to help themselves.

In the past, South African practice has been dominated, in the main, by the policy of establishing a European form of administration in the place of Native tribalism. Native Law and Custom might be recognized for purposes of convenience, but it was to be applied in almost every case by European Magistrates. This did not necessarily mean, however, that Native Courts ceased to function. In the Transvaal, for example, where the European Courts refused to hear cases concerning *lobola*, Native disputes as to marriage and inheritance were of necessity settled by the Chiefs, who arbitrated in civil matters in most other areas besides. Their jurisdiction was, however, extra-legal: it was not recognized, and, therefore, not controlled by Government.

Native Law and Custom is merely tribalism in its legal aspect, while the Chiefs' Courts represent tribalism in its judicial aspect. It is difficult to see why the one should merit recognition and control, and the other not. In the course of time, moreover, the European attitude towards tribalism underwent considerable change, in South Africa as elsewhere, and the view slowly gained ground that progress might best be assured by recognizing Native institutions, working through them, and using them as a point of departure for further development. [54]

This gradual change of outlook was reflected in a number of provisions of the Native Administration Act of 1927. Before considering these, however, it will be convenient to notice certain points in which the Act simplified and co-ordinated the administration of justice in general.

Native Law and Custom is given full recognition in the Courts of Native Commissioners, except in so far as it is opposed to the principles of public policy or natural justice. The Act specifically lays down, moreover, that the custom of *lobola* shall not be regarded as repugnant to these principles.

In recognition of the fact that Native Law is a growing, and not a static, body of rules, power was given to the Governor-General to amend the Natal Native Code by Proclamation. Advantage was soon taken of this provision, and a Revised Code, applicable to Natal and Zululand, made its appearance in 1932.

Another feature of the Act was the power it gave to Native Commissioners, whose Courts are competent to deal with almost all civil cases arising between Natives, to call in Native Assessors to advise them in matters relating to Native Law and Custom.

Appeals from the Courts of Native Commissioners are heard by two Native Appeal Courts, set up under the authority of the Act. Special provision is also made for dealing cheaply and expeditiously with divorce suits brought by Natives married under Christian rites or under the Civil Law.

More important, however, as an indication of a gradual change in policy, was the power given to the Governor-General to authorize any Chief or Headman to hear civil cases arising out of Native Law and Custom, if brought by a Native against a Native in his area. This authority has already been granted in several instances, notably to the Paramount Chiefs of Tembuland and Western Pondoland, and to four other principal Chiefs in the Transkeian Territories. An appeal lies from the Chief's Court to the Native Commissioner of the district.

The Governor-General may also grant to any Chief or Headman criminal jurisdiction, with power to fine up to two head of cattle or £5, over members of his own tribe residing on tribal land, in the case of offences punishable under Native Law and Custom. (55) While no territorial limit is set to this clause, it has only been applied as yet in Zululand and that part of the Cape Province known as British Bechuanaland where, it may be added, Chiefs have exercised civil and criminal jurisdiction since their country came under European control in 1885. Under the Natal Code of Native Law of 1932, moreover, Chiefs and Headmen have power to enforce obedience to authority, and may impose a fine not exceeding £2 for any defiance of their orders. (56)

The powers given by the Native Administration Act of 1927 were permissive only, and it is hardly surprising that relatively little use should have been made of them, as yet, by an administration steeped in the traditions of 'direct rule'. Moreover, although tribalism is still a living institution in most of the Reserves, its authority is very much on the wane amongst the great mass of Natives living on European land, while, in the urban areas, it is dying fast, if not already dead. It is obviously impossible to work through Native institutions where they have ceased to exist, and, even in predominantly tribal areas, there are a certain number of individuals who have adopted a European mode of life.

The question of the extent to which laws designed to meet the supposed needs of tribal Natives should be applied to the Europeanized minority had received some attention long before Union. As early as 1864 the principle of exempting certain Natives from the operation of Native Law and Custom had been recognized in Natal. [57] In the Cape, it is, broadly speaking, true to say that Natives registered as Parliamentary voters were excluded from the operation of differential legislation in 1887; [58] while in the Transvaal and the Free State, the practice of issuing letters of exemption, granting the holders immunity from the Pass Laws, was introduced in the early years of the present century. These various enactments were repealed by the Native Administration Act of 1927. In their place the Governor-General was given power to grant a letter of exemption to any Native freeing him, in whole or in part, from legislation specially affecting Natives, with the important exception, however, of laws regulating the ownership and occupation of land, the imposition of taxation, and the supply of liquor. (59) This power has been exercised in individual cases, but no standard mode of procedure has as yet been introduced.

7. *The council system*

The recognition of the possible value of Native institutions in the administrative sphere has come rather late, as it was only too frequently the policy, for close on a century, to destroy what many would now wish to see preserved. An attempt had, however, been made, in the eastern districts of the Cape, to find a partial substitute in the principle of consultation, embodied in the Council System. By 1903, thirteen districts were already included within the orbit of the Transkeian Territories General Council, and, some twenty years later, the number had increased to nineteen, including all the Native districts of the Transkei, Tembuland and East Griqualand.

As originally constituted, the District Councils were representative of the Headmen, though in those districts where the system of individual quit-rent tenure was applied, members were elected by the local ratepayers. The principle of election was extended to any district which might desire it as from the year 1913, and became general in 1925. Each District Council still has six members, of whom four are now chosen by the ratepayers, and two are nominated by the Governor-General, with the local Native Commissioner as Chairman. The District Council, in its turn, nominates two of its members, and the Governor-General appoints one additional member, to serve the district in the General Council.

In the Transkeian Territories, the Native inhabitants have thus come to be represented in the various Councils by elected members, and not by their traditional Chiefs as such. The principle of election by a majority count is, however, foreign to the Bantu mind, and when the Council system was introduced in Western Pondoland, in 1911, it had to be modified very considerably to meet the needs of a well-organized tribal society. Here, in fact, each District Council was composed of four members nominated by the Paramount Chief, and two appointed by the Governor-General, with a General Council for the four districts as a whole. The extension of the system to Eastern Pondoland, in 1927, involved yet another variant of the general pattern. For each of the three District Councils then established, two members are nominated by the local ratepayers, two by the Paramount Chief, and two by the Governor-General.

First applied to the four Western districts of the Transkei in 1895, the Council system was thus extended, in a little over a generation, to nineteen districts coming under the Transkeian Territories General Council, and to seven districts under the Pondoland General Council. The process of unification was finally completed by the amalgamation of these two bodies, under the name and style of the United Transkeian Territories General Council, as from January 1st, 1931.

The General Council, or *Bunga*, is the central feature of the system. It is composed of European administrative officers and Native members. The District Councils send their representatives, submit programmes of work for official sanction, and act as its local agents in carrying out approved schemes. The *Bunga* is, however, an advisory body only. It facilitates consultation with representative Natives, and provides a useful forum for the expression of opinion on a variety of topics. The annual reports of its proceedings are a mine of interesting information. Important matters are referred to Select Committees on education, accounts, laws and Native customs, land and stock, and these report to the full Council in due course. The conduct of debate is characterized by marked restraint, great respect for rules of procedure, and very considerable ability. The *Bunga*, in fact, provides an admirable training for its members, but its scope is limited, since 'administrative functions rest entirely with the Chief Magistrate'. (60) After the discussions in Council, this official, who is now styled Chief Native Commissioner, was in the habit of referring the questions at issue to an 'Official Conference', composed of the Native Commissioners of all the Council districts, to decide what action should be taken.

The revenue of the *Bunga* is derived from the proceeds of the local tax and quit rents collected in the Transkei, and transferred to it from the Native Development Account. Prior to the establishment of that fund, considerable expenditure had been incurred upon scholastic education, but the *Bunga* has been relieved of this burden since 1925, though a small provision is still made each year for scholarships. Its primary outgoings are in respect of public works, agricultural development and general administration. These activities necessitate a large establishment of Europeans and of Natives, employed and paid for by the Council. The Engineering Branch is responsible for the construction and maintenance of roads and bridges, advice on dam construction, and specifications for buildings. The Agricultural Development Branch maintains a number of demonstration farms, and three agricultural schools, the first of which was founded in 1913. Vocational instruction is provided, and pupils are trained as agricultural demonstrators. The *Bunga* has already engaged approximately a hundred of these for work in the districts. Their activities are supervised by the Director of Agriculture, an official of the *Bunga*, who is responsible for anti-soil-erosion schemes, fencing, plantations and other undertakings of vital concern for the future of the

Territories. Small grants are also made to local hospitals, and a considerable amount of administrative work is performed by Council officials.

The following table shows the total revenue and expenditure of the various Council districts, now included under the United Transkeian Territories General Council, since 1903: (61)

Expenditure	1. vii. 1903 to 30. vi. 1932	Estimates 1932–3
	£	£
Establishments	128,934	7,645
Education	466,697	1,550
Agriculture	870,338	59,649
Public Works	918,910	64,019
Public Health	59,977	5,920
Other	221,354	11,455
Total	2,666,210	150,238
Revenue	2,686,311	148,336

In addition to these activities, the *Bunga* has undertaken stock dipping on a large scale. This has been financed, since 1915, by the levy of special stock rates, and involves a considerable establishment, both Native and European. The work has been a marked success, but this very fact has served to intensify the problem of over-stocking, which is no less a menace in the Transkei than in other Native areas of Africa outside the fly belt.

The General Council has already done much to improve agricultural conditions and to foster Native welfare. It has also developed a political sense in those Natives who take part in its activities, and has made them wish for more than a merely advisory rôle in the framing of policy. In course of time, indeed, they came to realize that the *Bunga* itself—housed in new and commodious buildings since 1928—was little more than an imposing façade, and that the real power was vested in the Official Conference of Magistrates. The demand for a more intimate participation in the work of Government grew steadily more persistent, and finally led to an official promise of a revised Constitution at the time of the amalgamation of all the Transkeian Territories under one General Council. A special committee, composed of Magistrates and Native members, was set up to investigate the matter, and its proposals, with some modifications introduced by the Government, were embodied in a Proclamation issued in 1932.

Membership of the various Councils remains as it was, save that the principle of partial election, established in Eastern Pondoland, is now extended to Western Pondoland, and that the Paramount Chiefs of Eastern and Western Pondoland are *ex officio* members of the General Council. The really significant innovation, however, is the establishment of an Executive Committee, consisting of the Chief Native Commissioner—who is and remains the

Chief Executive Officer of the General Council—
together with three Native Commissioners, and four
Native members appointed on the nomination of
the *Bunga*. The Committee is responsible for the
administration and control of important Council
affairs relating to establishments, education, agriculture and public works, though the Chairman has
the right to deal with any urgent business, provided
he report his action to the Committee in due course,
and may also reserve any question for decision by
the Minister. (62) This arrangement is, of course, far
from giving full executive powers to the Native
members of the *Bunga*, but it does bring their representatives into the inner counsels of government,
and is an interesting development of the principle
of consultation.

By implication, the Proclamation extends the
advisory powers of the General Council beyond the
geographical limits of the Transkeian Territories.
The *Bunga* may now initiate and consider 'any
matter relating to the economic, industrial or social
condition of the Native population of the Union or
any part thereof', and discuss 'any proposed legislation or existing law which specially affects the
Native population of the Union'—in either case 'in
so far as it affects the Natives within the area of the
jurisdiction of the Council'. (63) Within these limits,
important no doubt in theory but difficult to define
in practice, the United Transkeian Territories
General Council has become a forum for the ex-

pression of opinion on Native policy as a whole. These innovations are fraught with many interesting possibilities, but are as yet too recent to have made any appreciable difference in the working of the Council system.

From early days the Transkei has developed on lines of its own, and its Councils are perhaps the most interesting contribution South Africa has yet made in the field of Native policy. The extension of the system elsewhere has not, however, met with anything like the same success. The Native Affairs Act of 1920 empowered the Governor-General, on the recommendation of the Native Affairs Commission, to establish local Councils in any Native area. Unlike their Transkeian prototype, these Councils are to consist of Native members only, though an officer in the public service may be appointed to preside at their meetings, and to act in an advisory capacity towards them. (64) For one reason or another none was established until 1927. Meanwhile an amending Act had been passed, which aimed at the creation of local Councils with lesser powers than those originally contemplated. (65) Up to the present, eight Councils have been set up with full powers, and a like number with restricted powers. (66) The Act of 1920 also envisaged the creation of General Councils, with jurisdiction over two or more local Council areas, but this section has not as yet been applied in actual practice. In most parts of the Union, Native areas are too scattered to make such a scheme feasible, and development in this direction must therefore wait upon the solution of the central problem of the land.

8. *Native policy in the union*

Hitherto we have considered, in outline, the official attitude of the Union of South Africa towards the more important individual aspects of Native policy. It remains to see what light this set of separate solutions may throw upon Native policy as a whole. Unfortunately, however, it is not possible to place the subject in its proper statistical setting, for the Native and Coloured population were not included in the Census taken in 1931. As it is essential to attempt to indicate the numerical strength of the various sections of the population, recourse must be had to guesswork, which may be very wide of the mark. It will be assumed that the total population of the Union is in the neighbourhood of eight millions, and that it is made up, in round figures, somewhat as follows:

White	1,800,000
Black	5,500,000
Coloured	600,000
Asiatic	200,000
Total	8,100,000

For simplicity's sake, the Coloured population will be left out of the picture. It provides what is, admittedly, a most important, though, in the main, a local problem for the Western and Central portions of the Cape Province, where there are relatively few Blacks. The Asiatics, for their part, are largely concentrated in the lower-lying areas of Natal, and do not as yet much influence the Union as a whole. The major issue is the relationship between less than two million Whites and more than five million Blacks.

Pursuing these dangerous approximations still further, one may hazard a guess that the Black population is distributed more or less in the following manner:

In the Native areas	2,500,000
In other rural areas	2,200,000
In towns	800,000
Total	5,500,000

The Abantu are essentially a peasant people, but less than half have anything like a secure footing on the land, while a growing proportion is becoming urbanized. Even the Reserves are dependent upon the mines, where scores of thousands of their younger manhood are forced, by economic pressure, to seek employment each year. On the one hand, there is the land hunger of the masses: on the other, the advent of a tiny, but important fraction of Bantu 'intellectuals'. (67)

When one turns to the European population, one is on somewhat surer ground. Slightly under one-half speak English as the Mother tongue, and slightly over one-half Afrikaans. Of the latter, however, close on one-third—say 300,000—live at or below the minimum essential to a European standard of living, and are either 'Poor Whites', or in great danger of becoming so. (68) The ominous fact of the degeneracy of a growing proportion of those Europeans whose families have been longest in the country is only too relevant to the 'native' question in South Africa. Behind the scenes, comparatively rarely expressed, but hardly ever forgotten, is the realization that, while a considerable portion of the White population is sinking, a not inconsiderable number of the Blacks are rising in the economic and social scale.

It will at once be apparent that the background of Native policy in the Union is utterly different from that of any other British territory in Africa—if we make a very partial exception of Kenya and the Rhodesias, where, however, the issues inherent in White settlement have hitherto been largely covered in a cloak of optimism. Nor should it be forgotten that, in parts, at least, of the Union, the European population arrived before the Abantu. These facts should arouse sympathy without, however, dulling the critical faculties. For an outsider the only comment truly apposite would seem to be the classic phrase of Abraham Lincoln, when speaking, in

1854, on the then burning issue of slavery: 'I surely will not blame them [i.e. the Southerners] for not doing what I should not know how to do myself'.

For a satisfactory solution of the Native problem, as of any other, mutual goodwill is essential. On the European side it is pleasant to record a growing interest in Native questions, more especially among the younger generation of the Universities, be the language Afrikaans or English. Moreover, organizations like the Joint Councils which exist in many towns, and the South African Institute of Race Relations, are doing much to focus the attention of people of goodwill upon this very pressing human problem. It would be idle to pretend, however, that genuine co-operation between all races in the interest of South Africa as a whole were even an ideal, however remote, to the majority of the electorate. On the Native side, there is a marked suspicion of the White man and all his ways, which is by no means confined to the educated few. The emotional background is not so promising as it might be on either side.

The most important principle upon which the Native policy of the Union appears to be based is the distinction drawn between Natives living in the Reserves and those outside. The former have nearly all been brought under the direct control of the Department of Native Affairs. Where they are concerned, the Executive has a general power of legislation by Proclamation; in many cases these Natives have a share in the management of their own affairs through local Councils; they are virtually exempt from the operation of the Pass Laws; their tribal customs have received a considerable measure of recognition; their traditional leaders have a minor executive rôle to perform, and, in some cases, now exercise judicial powers as well. It is, moreover, an established principle that no non-Native may acquire land in the Reserves. Here, then, the principle of 'possessory segregation' operates in favour of the Native.

Outside the Reserves the position is very different. The Natives are usually within the jurisdiction of officials of the Department of Justice; they are subject more directly to Parliamentary control, and any exercise of the power of legislation by Proclamation over them is limited to matters specified by statute. The Native has to conform to a series of restrictions from which other classes of society are exempt; he has virtually no share in local government, apart from the Location Boards recently established in certain municipal areas: and he is, in practice, either debarred from acquiring land altogether, or may only do so with the consent of the Governor-General. This is, of course, not the case in the Cape Province, where Natives may even qualify for the Parliamentary Franchise; while, in urban areas throughout the Union, the principle of residential segregation is gradually being applied, with exceptions usually designed to suit the convenience of Europeans. In the main, however, it may be said that whereas, in the Reserves, Native development is encouraged as such, outside the Reserves, the Native exists very largely on sufferance. He is treated as a foreign body, useful, no doubt, but rather a menace to a civilization more splendid than his own.

The distinction has an approximate basis in geography. From the South Western and Central regions of the Cape, through the Free State to the Southern Transvaal, and including the Northern portions of Natal, is a temperate zone of hill and valley rising past the Karroo to the high veld. Reserves are almost non-existent, and if Natives come in to work, they do so on the White Man's terms. They cannot hope to own land in this belt, save in the Cape, for here, in practice, the principle of possessory segregation operates in favour of the European. It is almost an article of faith that the backbone of the Union must be White. The ultimate feasibility of this basic principle will doubtless depend upon the extent to which the European South African will be able to cultivate his land himself. It would seem to imply, as a corollary, however, the adequate provision of land for Natives elsewhere, and this has not yet been made.

The Reserves as at present constituted are admittedly inadequate. Almost equally unfortunate is the manner in which they are being exploited by a growing Native population. The Abantu are devoted to their cattle, which they regard in terms of numbers rather than of quality. Cattle are for them the principal store of wealth; they form the traditional consideration in *lobola*; they are the outward and visible symbol of a primitive outlook on life which is reinforced by the sanctions of religion and society. Improved veterinary services lead to an increase in the number of cattle; over-stocking leads to over-grazing, and this, in its turn, speeds up the dangerous course of soil erosion. The introduction of more modern methods of agriculture would demand a fundamental change in the Bantu attitude towards cattle, and therefore towards life itself. This can only come by persuasion, for which more and better facilities for education are indispensable. A permanent solution would also necessitate considerable capital expenditure for the provision of fencing and minor irrigation works. The saving of the natural resources of the Reserves is, however, as clearly a national service as is the release of White farmers from the burden of excessive interest charges, or the financing of anti-soil-erosion schemes on land in European ownership. It is also a matter of great urgency, as the Native Economic Commission very clearly showed in its Report. (69) Unless action is taken soon, the Reserves will become still less adequate to support their population, and this would be a serious blow to all—Europeans and Natives alike.

If one assume a policy of economic development in the Reserves, together with the adequate provision of additional land for Native occupation, it is perhaps conceivable that White and Black may ultimately work on parallel lines in agriculture. When, however, one turns to enterprises common to the country as a whole, like transport, or to that superb milch cow, the Rand, upon which almost everything else at present depends, it is not easy to see how the principle of racial differentiation can be applied without causing gross injustice and even grosser inefficiency. Since 1927 the Government has steadily pursued the policy of substituting Poor Whites for Blacks in the lower grades of labour on the Railways. It has been an expensive process, and does not appear to have brought a solution of the Poor White problem appreciably nearer. The principle of the Colour Bar in industry, which received statutory recognition in 1926, [70] is enforced, in actual practice, more by Trade Union action than by Government Regulations. In so far as European labour is, in many grades, more expensive than Native, it has the effect of raising the cost of production; strengthening claims to higher protective duties; and adding to the cost of living. Thus many industries, first encouraged in the very proper hope of making South Africa less exclusively dependent upon its mines, can only flourish so long as prosperity on the Rand pours purchasing power throughout the land.

However much one may regret the fact, a large number of Natives are already industrialized. If, therefore, it is the policy of the Union to foster the employment of Whites and Coloured persons in transport and industry, to the exclusion of Natives, some alternative outlet must obviously be found for them. This points, amongst other things, once again to the provision of more land. It is not a question of righting an historic wrong: the past is past. It might indeed be argued that Black men, as such, have no more inherent right to land than White men, as such, and there is certainly a large and growing class of landless Whites. Moreover, no sane person would criticize the desire to find a place for the Poor Whites in the economic life of the country, however much he may doubt the wisdom, and regret the political character, of some of the experiments hitherto attempted on their behalf. The principal conclusion would rather seem to be that the problems facing any racial section of this heterogeneous community can only be solved in terms of the community as a whole.

To an outsider it would appear that, apart from its mineral resources, the chief economic asset of the Union was its supply of cheap Native labour. These workers could soon become at once more efficient and more prosperous, to the advantage of all sections: but there is a very real danger of exploitation, and the undue depression of wage rates in general, so long as various forms of economic pressure, and, more especially, the inadequacy of available supplies of land, force rural Natives to the towns. Once again one realizes the tragic consequences of failure to implement the intentions of the Natives Land Act of 1913.

The present is a critical time in the history of Native policy in the Union. There has been a flavour of repression in certain enactments of the past, and the test of colour has sometimes been substituted for that of quality. This has been to the abiding advantage of no section of the community—as witness the present parlous condition of the Poor Whites—still less to that of the Union as a whole. Fortunately, however, there are signs of a new outlook on the part of many representative South Africans. It is coming to be realized that, in its divergences of race and colour, the Union is faced with problems more difficult perhaps than those of any other country in the world. The ultimate solution cannot be cast into the mould of a formula, even though it bear the magic name of segregation. (71) It will depend upon the future development of all the races in the land, and this is in the womb of time. But first things can be taken first, and an equitable solution of the question of the land, even at some considerable financial sacrifice, would be an admirable beginning. It would relieve the present economic pressure, and make it easier for White and Black to go their several ways in many fields of life, with each in harmony of end with all. It would help to create an atmosphere of goodwill, and thus bring nearer to realization the splendid motto of the youthful State itself: *Ex Unitate Vires.*

PART II

THE HIGH COMMISSION TERRITORIES

9. *Introduction*

OUTSIDE the political frontiers of the Union of South Africa, but closely bound up with it in the economic sphere, are three predominantly Native territories which, by an accident of history, still remain under the direct control of the British Government. Basutoland is an enclave in the Union: the vast expanses of the Bechuanaland Protectorate form a corridor between the Cape Province and the Zambezi: while little Swaziland lies tucked away between Natal, the Transvaal, and Portuguese East Africa. Each of these countries is administered by a Resident Commissioner, under the High Commissioner for South Africa, who is responsible, in his turn, to the Dominions Office in Downing Street. Some relevant facts—or conjectural approximations, as the case may be—are summarized in the table on the next page. Here is a population of under a million, nearly all of whom are Blacks, spread in a most irregular fashion over an area of close on 300,000 square miles. Its density varies from several hundred to the square mile in some of the valleys of Basutoland, to almost nothing in the wilds of the Kalahari.

Administrative policy in these territories has been greatly influenced by an underlying feeling of uncertainty as to their ultimate political destiny. Although they were not included in the Union, the South Africa Act established procedure, and indicated conditions, for their transfer in the future. (1) This fact in itself gives the present regime something of a provisional flavour, but Native opinion in all

	Area (thousand sq. miles)			Census population, 1921 (thousands)		Probable population, 1933 (thousands)	
	Total	Reserves	European Land	Black	White	Total	Per sq. mile
Basutoland	11·7	11·7	—	493	1·5	580	50
Bechuanaland	275·0	102·0	7·5	150	1·6	200	¾
Swaziland	6·7	2·7	3·8	110	2·2	125	19

three territories is unanimous in opposing incorporation, if in nothing else.

The economic position of the territories operates as a further limiting factor. In 1910 they entered into a Customs Agreement with the Union of South Africa. From a revenue point of view, this arrangement has probably been, on the whole, to their advantage. (2) It has, however, had the effect of applying to these countries the tariff policy of the Union, which is certainly not designed to meet the needs of backward Native territories. Moreover,

the Witwatersrand is practically the only outlet for
the cattle of Bechuanaland and Basutoland, while
Swaziland tobacco is also dependent upon the Union
for its market. Wool and mohair from Basutoland
are almost the only important products which find
their way overseas. The rapid growth of population
during the present century has led to congestion in
the kraals, and made them increasingly dependent
upon the annual migration of their young manhood
to the mines. Under these conditions it is clearly
most difficult for the British authorities to evolve
an independent policy of economic development,
while uncertainty as to the future hinders initiative
in other spheres besides. The motto of the administration, in all three territories, has thus tended to be
Quieta non movere, an outlook which is also ex-
plainable in part by the manner in which they
originally came under the control of the Crown.

10. *Basutoland*

The Basuto are a Bantu-speaking people who became a nation in the nineteenth century under the
leadership of Moshesh, one of the outstanding Native
rulers of Africa. The advent of Dutch settlers beyond
the Orange River, however, led to the cession of
some of their best land, and even threatened their
independence in the mountain fastnesses which had
perforce become their home. Moshesh therefore
turned to Great Britain for support, and was finally

admitted, in 1868, into the allegiance of Her Majesty.
The British Government was not enthusiastic about
its new acquisition, which it had made solely 'with
a view to the restoration of peace and the future
maintenance of tranquillity and good government
on the North Eastern Border of the Colony of the
Cape of Good Hope'. (3) In 1869 the frontier line
between Basutoland and the Free State was settled
by agreement, and two years later the territory was
annexed to the Cape Colony.

The period of colonial rule was marked by a
number of errors of judgment. Zealous Magistrates
rigidly applied European conceptions of law in
tribal matters, while a premature proposal to double
the poll tax, and an ill-timed attempt to disarm the
people, finally led to open revolt in 1880. The military operations which followed were badly carried
out, and some of the burgher levies proved unre-
liable in face of the enemy. The Colony, weary of
commitments it seemed unable to fulfil, petitioned
the Home Government to undertake the responsibility in its stead. In 1884, therefore, albeit most
unwillingly, Imperial control was assumed over the
country, with the acquiescence of the Basuto themselves, and all legislative and executive authority
was vested in the High Commissioner. (4)

The local administration was placed under a
Resident Commissioner, with headquarters at
Maseru. The first holder of this office was instructed
to see that expenditure should not exceed revenue.

though for a number of years he was able to count upon an annual grant from the Cape Colony. He was also to take all measures necessary for the protection of life and property, and the maintenance of order on the border. One of the principal tasks of the small European administrative staff was the institution of internal self-government amongst the Basuto, who were to be responsible, so far as possible, for the suppression of crime and the settlement of inter-tribal disputes. A solution of this problem was greatly simplified, from the European point of view, by the fact that all the tribes recognized the paramountcy of the house of Moshesh. The tribal organization of the Basuto had successfully resisted the various interferences to which it had been subjected during the colonial period. It was henceforward recognized as an integral part of the government machine.

In the administration of justice, British Courts were set up to try cases involving Europeans, and also the more serious crimes committed by Natives. Most of the judicial work was, however, left to Native Courts. These were already in existence when British rule was first established, and the Regulations issued in 1884 aimed at their official recognition. It was then declared to be lawful for any Native Chief, appointed by the Resident Commissioner, to adjudicate upon and try such cases, criminal or civil, and to exercise jurisdiction in such manner and within such limits, as might be defined by any rules established by the authority of the Resident Commissioner. (5) In actual practice, there has been very little regulation or control, and the Native Courts have been largely left to work out their own salvation in their own way. This has tended to stereotype these institutions on antiquated lines. The number of Chiefs' Courts appears to be excessive, and continues to increase. Appeals to the Court of the Paramount Chief involve considerable delay and unnecessary expense, though the institution of Native Circuit Courts of Appeal has recently helped to speed up the process. After nearly fifty years of British rule, there is, however, no provision for the keeping of a written record of cases in any of these Courts, while Court fines are still regarded as a perquisite of the Chiefs.

An attempt was made, in 1929, to remedy these defects on lines adopted with conspicuous success in other parts of British Africa. Unfortunately, however, the way was not sufficiently prepared. The programme of reform aroused the opposition of the Chiefs, and was quietly shelved. At present, therefore, the Courts continue to function much as before, though they have lost something of the confidence and the esteem of the more progressive elements of Native society.

So long as the Basutoland administration was in receipt of an annual grant from the Cape, it virtually

invited outside criticism, and was also prevented
from building up a reserve fund. The implications
of the situation were brought home to the people
by Sir Alfred Milner, when he visited the country in
1898. As a result, the Chiefs voluntarily agreed to
an increase in the poll tax from 10s. to 20s. Since
that time Basutoland has been self-supporting,
though it was necessary to raise the tax to 25s. in
1920. This is the rate in force at the present time.
It is payable by each adult male, and also in
respect of each wife, after the first, up to a total
of three. There is, in addition, a special levy
of 3s., which is earmarked for expenditure on
education.

The collection of the direct tax was originally
entrusted to the Chiefs. They were relieved of this
duty in 1905, and it is now collected by Government
agents who are, however, assisted in their task by
the Chiefs or their representatives. In addition to
the tax payable to Government, the Basuto have
certain obligations towards the Chiefs, who may call
upon them to take messages or to cultivate their
lands. (6) Service of this nature was originally
limited to four days a year, but seems to have increased during the present century.

In earlier days, the Basuto Chiefs had occasionally
met together to consider matters of great common
interest. This afforded a precedent for the institution

of a Council, and, in 1903, the Chiefs readily agreed to hold meetings for the discussion of tribal affairs, in consultation with the Government. A forum was thus provided for the ventilation of grievances, and also for an informal exchange of views on such matters as the appropriation of money paid in taxes. The experiment was successful, and in 1910 the National Council was officially recognized by Proclamation. (7) It meets each year under the presidency of the Resident Commissioner, but its other members are all Natives. They number a hundred, including the Paramount Chief and ninety-four persons nominated by him, together with five others appointed by the Resident Commissioner. The Basutoland Council is thus much more markedly Native and tribal in character than the General Council of the United Transkeian Territories. It is composed almost exclusively of Chiefs, and is usually very conservative in outlook. In this it is probably representative of the great majority of the people, though hardly at all of the small but steadily growing minority of educated Natives.

The Council has frequently discussed problems relating to Native Law and Custom. It even made a small compilation, so long ago as 1903, called the 'Basutoland Native Laws of Lerotholi', after the then Paramount Chief. This code, which was an entirely Native product, was amended by the Council in 1922. It is not recognized by Government as having the force of law, though, as a statement of existing custom, it has considerable influence upon the practice of the Native Courts.

The Council is an advisory body, but its opinion carries great weight with the Administration. This was clearly shown in 1929, when the determined opposition of its members led to the withdrawal of a draft Proclamation defining the relations and duties existing between the Administration and the Chiefs, and between the Chiefs and the people under their authority. With a view to increasing the representative character of Council members, Assistant-Commissioners have recently encouraged them to hold gatherings (*Pitso*) in their districts for the discussion of questions which may afterwards be raised in the National Council.

In the long run, the institution of chieftainship can only survive if it adapt itself to changing conditions, and, in this admittedly difficult process, some measure of European guidance is essential. The relative absence of initiative in this respect must therefore be conceded as a blot to critics of the British regime. [8]

In the field of education and public health, however, Basutoland can safely invite comparison with any Native territory in Africa, even though it be admitted, here as elsewhere, that not every item of expenditure is always well conceived. Moreover, on the educational side, the country has certainly been fortunate in its missionaries. The Paris Evangelical Society arrived so long ago as 1859, and counted some very remarkable men amongst its pioneers. The Roman Catholics, for their part, are represented by the Oblate Fathers and the Marist Brothers, two experienced organizations which have also long years of devoted labour to their credit, and are now better equipped and more active than ever before. If an overwhelming majority of the schools is run by the Missions, it must not be assumed that Government is indifferent in the matter of education. It is directly responsible for the Lerotholi Technical School at Maseru, and for three intermediate schools. It makes a small annual grant to the South African Native College at Fort Hare, and large annual grants to the mission schools in the country itself. In the year 1931–2, expenditure on Native education amounted to approximately 19 per cent. of total expenditure, and was greater than that incurred on police and prisons. In the same year, expenditure on medical services, together with that on the somewhat expensive leper settlement near Maseru, accounted for over 16 per cent. of the total outgoings of the Colony. To place these figures in proper perspective, it may be useful to compare them with the estimates, made by the Native Economic Commission, of expenditure incurred on Native account in the Union of South Africa for the financial year 1929–30. (9) Adopting these figures, South African expenditure on education, Union and Provincial, may be calculated at a little under 14½ per cent., and that on public health and mental and other hospitals at over 11 per cent. of the total expenditure charged to Natives. It is interesting to notice, moreover, that the cost of police and prisons incurred on behalf of the Native population was well over double that of Native education. This comparison should obviously not be pressed too far, but it does suggest that the administration of Basutoland is not behind in the financial provision it already makes for Native welfare.

The greatest difficulty facing the Colony is an economic one. The population is increasing fast, while soil erosion is probably proceeding still faster. Hideous dongas scar the countryside, and much good land is washed away each season to the sea. The menace, familiar enough in other Native areas, is particularly serious here. To combat it successfully would need considerable expenditure on capital account. This is also required for new roads, for without better means of transport, it is unlikely that much progress can be made in the marketing of wool and other products. It will, moreover, be hard to make any really serious improvement in Native agricultural methods without some substantial modification in the present system of landholding. In these and other directions there is need for greater initiative, and for the adoption of a long period policy of economic development. It is, however, hard to see how any real progress can be achieved until some definite decision is arrived at as to the future status of the Colony itself.

11. *Bechuanaland*

Bechuanaland offers a marked contrast to Basutoland. It is a vast territory with very little land really suitable for agriculture or stock-raising on improved lines.   In Basutoland all the land is tribal: in Bechuanaland there are Native Reserves, blocks alienated to Europeans, and an enormous tract of unalienated Crown land.   Covetous eyes are sometimes cast on the Protectorate by those who see in it an outlet for the surplus Native population of the Union, or for the settlement of Poor Whites.   Its suitability for any such purpose is, however, more than doubtful.   After rain the country becomes a smiling garden, but periods of reasonable precipitation are almost invariably followed by still longer periods of drought.   Even in the better watered areas, agriculture is limited to the growing of subsistence crops, and these are frequently inadequate. Much of Bechuanaland may best be described as 'marginal ranching country'.   In the Ngami and Ghansi districts pasture is more abundant, but poor supplies of drinking water and the remoteness of the area combine to make development difficult, if not impossible.   By an unfortunate provision of Providence, the better watered country round the

Okavango delta is infested with tsetse fly, and is thus impossible for cattle. (10)

The Bechuana tribes are Bantu speakers who claim a common ancestry, though they are now split up into eight groups, five of which are of fair importance. Each has a Chief of its own, but none has any claim to paramountcy over the others. The Bechuana came to the country as conquerors in relatively recent times, and proceeded to establish their authority over the peoples they found there, or over those who sought refuge amongst them at a later date. The result is that the population of the tribal areas is by no means homogeneous, the subordinate tribes including such interesting relics as the Masarwa, who are more or less pure Bushmen, and a certain number of Hottentots in the remoter regions of the Kalahari. In some cases the ruling tribesmen form but a small proportion of the total. Thus, in Khama's country, the Bamangwato probably do not represent more than one-fifth of the population, and the status of the despised Masarwa in their midst is not exactly in accord with that principle of trusteeship which most educated Bechuana would doubtless wish to see applied, by Europeans, to themselves.

The first White men to influence the Bechuana were the missionaries—and the London Missionary Society has the distinction of counting Robert

Moffat and David Livingstone amongst its early
pioneers in this part of Africa—but political pene-
tration had to wait for the advent of Cecil Rhodes.
To him, Bechuanaland was 'the great trade route
into the interior', and its possession was essential, if
the Cape Colony were ever to become 'the dominant
State of South Africa'. To ensure expansion of this
type, there seemed at first to be no room for 'the
Imperial factor in Bechuanaland', but this position
Rhodes soon surrendered, in view of the annexation-
ist designs of the South African Republic. Under
pressure from the Cape, and in the fear that Dutch
and German might join hands, Great Britain went
so far, in 1885, as to annex the country which is still
known as British Bechuanaland and now forms part
of the Cape Province, and to declare a Protectorate
over the territory extending from North of Mafeking
to the Zambezi. Four years later this protected zone
was included in what was officially described, in its
Charter of Incorporation, as the principal field of
the operations of the British South Africa Company,
though it remained, for the time being, under an
Assistant Commissioner appointed by the Crown.
The leading Native Chiefs of the Protectorate took
fright at the prospect of Company rule, and at the
possible alternative of incorporation in the Cape.
Under missionary guidance, Khama of the Bamangwato, Bathoen of the Bangwaketsi, and Sebele of
the Bakwena went to England, in 1895, to see the
Queen. Clad, as the custom then was, in top hat and

frock coat, these potentates soon acquired a publicity value, and the arrangement they reached with Joseph Chamberlain has influenced British administration in the Protectorate down to the present day.

It was agreed to set aside a narrow strip of territory to the East for the construction of a railway line from Mafeking to Bulawayo. Apart from this, the Chiefs were each to 'have a country within which they shall live, as hitherto, under the protection of the Queen', who will appoint an officer to reside with them. 'The Chiefs will rule their own people much as at present. The Queen's officer will decide all cases in which White men, or Black men who do not belong to the tribe of one of the three Chiefs, are concerned, or in which the punishment is death. He will also have a right to hear an appeal in any very serious case, even if the punishment is short of death. The people under the Chiefs shall pay a hut tax, or tax of a similar nature, but, as the Chiefs wish it, they may collect it—at all events for the present—themselves and pay it over to the Queen's officer, but this is not to be made a reason for paying over too little'. The agreement also envisaged the establishment of a police force, Native and European; aimed at the suppression of all traffic in strong drink; and at a final settlement of tribal boundaries. (11)

Any possibility of a transfer of the administration to the Chartered Company was brought to an end by the Jameson raid, which took place soon after. This did not, of course, affect the railway concession, and, by 1897, a line ran through the land from South to North. The introduction of modern transport facilities was, however, only of importance to the eastern fringe of the Protectorate, where the ceded strip passed into the possession of the British South Africa Company in 1904, and thus became available for European settlement. Meanwhile a careful study had been made of tribal claims to land, and a large tract of country was set aside for the exclusive occu- pation of Natives in 1899. (12) With a few minor changes in boundary, these Reserves still exist as they were then constituted. In 1910, the remainder of the country was declared to be Crown land, (13) but no steps have yet been taken to alienate any part of it. On the North Eastern frontier, however, land and mineral rights over upwards of two thou- sand square miles are vested in the Tati Company, under a concession acquired from the Amandebele in 1887. Outside this district, the position as to minerals is somewhat complicated, though it may be summarized by saying that, with one or two relatively minor exceptions, the Chartered Company holds exclusive prospecting rights in certain areas, and a general preferential claim, valid as against other Europeans, but not yet clearly defined, in the remainder of the Protectorate.

Up to the present, mineral development has been on a very limited scale and the economic life of the country is still centred on cattle, together with a little subsistence farming. European settlement is virtually limited to the eastern border. It has not been, on the whole, a great success, and in some areas the Poor White problem has already come, apparently, to stay.

In the main, Bechuanaland is a Native territory, where progress is hindered by the familiar Bantu attitude towards cattle, and by the shortage of water. Education might help to change the one, and the boring of wells would perhaps do something, in certain areas at least, to solve the other. But both would cost money, and the financial resources of the country are very limited.

The principal items of revenue are the hut tax, and receipts from customs and excise. The latter consist almost exclusively of a small fixed percentage of the total revenue of the customs' administration of South Africa, (14) while the former can only be paid so long as the Native finds an outlet, either for his cattle or his labour, in the Union. The direct tax was fixed, in 1909, at 20s., payable in respect of every hut occupied by a Native. It has, however, the character of a poll tax in that, if two or more adult males live in one hut, each must pay his 20s., a sum which is also payable for every wife after the first. (15) In 1919 a Native Fund was established, into which are paid the proceeds of an additional levy of 5*s.* on every 20*s.* of hut tax due. The income of the Fund is expended for such purposes as Native education, the abatement of contagious diseases, and the improvement of Native cattle. (16) In 1932 the hut tax was raised to 23*s.*, but, in view of economic conditions, it was reduced to 10*s.* in 1933, plus, in each case, an additional 5*s.* levy for the Native Fund. (17) The rate may not appear unduly high, but the people are desperately poor. The problem is, moreover, complicated by the fact that the tax is still collected, in the main, through the agency of the Chiefs. This is done with success in many parts of British Tropical Africa, but, in Bechuanaland, no adequate control seems yet to have been devised to check abuses otherwise inevitable.

In the early days of British rule, the Protectorate depended upon an Imperial grant-in-aid which averaged £40,000 a year from 1899 to 1912. Thereafter careful administration during a period of comparative prosperity enabled the country to be self-supporting. More recently, however, expenditure has risen steadily, and three successive years of drought, coinciding with the temporary cessation of income-tax payments by the Rhodesia Railways in respect of their line through the territory, and culminating in an outbreak of foot and mouth disease, have brought the country to the verge of bankruptcy. In the financial year 1933–4, it received an Imperial grant-in-aid of no less than £177,000, and further assistance is necessary in 1934–5. These sums are required to meet current charges, and only a relatively small proportion is being spent on capital account.

One of the greatest difficulties of the Protectorate is that of finding a market for its cattle. In 1924 the Union Government imposed a minimum weight of 800 lbs. for oxen sent from Bechuanaland to Johannesburg, and this was raised to 1000 lbs. two years later. The full effect of these measures was not felt at the time because, during the construction period, the copper mines of Northern Rhodesia absorbed a welcome number of Bechuana beasts, while an outlet was also found in the cold storage market at Durban. All this was stopped by the epidemic of foot and mouth disease, and the consequent prohibition of cattle movements over the border, which came early in 1933. This state of affairs will, of course, not last for ever, but it will be difficult to recapture markets for these rather inferior beasts, if only on account of the certain opposition of European stock farmers in the countries concerned. The only hope would seem to lie in the provision of more wells and the establishment of a factory for meat products. (18) The effect of the eclipse of the main industry of the country is made still more serious in that the Bechuana, like the Zulu, but unlike the Basuto, do not take kindly, as a general rule, to labour in the mines.

In view of this somewhat gloomy background, it is not surprising that expenditure on Native welfare should have been severely circumscribed. In the financial year 1931–2, when the crisis was only beginning, total expenditure stood at £162,560, as against a corresponding revenue of only £106,735. Ordinary expenditure amounted to £135,012, of which the administration accounted for close on 18 per cent., and the police for some 22 per cent., as against an outlay on veterinary services of 13 per cent., on medical work of over 9 per cent., and on education of under 4 per cent. The vast size of the country, and the scattered nature of its population inevitably make administration relatively expensive, and limit the possibilities of Native development. In the absence of potentialities at present unforeseen, the Bechuanaland Protectorate offers an economic problem more difficult, perhaps, than that of any other British territory in Africa, with the possible exception of Somaliland. There are not even funds enough to make an administrative capital in the country itself, and headquarters must perforce remain at Mafeking, in Union territory.

Apparently uninfluenced by economic stress, the tribal structure of society is still, to outward semblance, much as it was in 1885. Beneath the surface, however, forces are at work which slowly make for change, and this in spite of years of relative inaction on the part of the administration. The official attitude was first defined in 1891, when an Order-in-Council instructed the High Commissioner, as chief local representative of the Crown, to 'respect any Native laws or customs by which the civil relations of any Native Chiefs, tribes or populations under Her Majesty's protection are now regulated, except so far as the same may be incompatible with the due exercise of Her Majesty's power and jurisdiction'. (19) European Courts were set up, but their jurisdiction was not to extend to any matter in which Natives only were concerned, save in the interests of peace, or for the prevention or punishment of acts of violence to person or property. (20) Five years later, however, these Courts were granted jurisdiction, in civil and criminal suits, over and against all persons residing within their respective areas. At the same time, murder cases were reserved to the Resident Commissioner, though they were transferred, in 1912, to the newly-established Special Court of the Protectorate. (21) Any Native Chief who might wish to exercise jurisdiction under the Proclamation of 1891 could be appointed to do so. In fact, the Chiefs continued to enjoy judicial powers, except in murder cases, much as they had done before, although, in theory, the European Magistrates had concurrent jurisdiction.

The position of Europeans in this scheme of things remained a trifle anomalous. At first no Native Court could try a case in which a European was involved, save with the consent of all the parties concerned, but, in 1922, such cases were excluded from their jurisdiction altogether. (22)

In general, the administration was loth to interfere with Native tribalism. It was not, indeed, till 1919 that procedure was introduced for appeals from the decisions of Native Courts. Even then the appeal was, somewhat strangely, made to lie to a Court composed of the Magistrate and of the Chief in question, and, should they disagree, then to the Resident Commissioner. (23) With the growth of missionary influence, it became, however, apparent that causes arising out of Native marriages contracted under Christian or civil rites could not adequately be decided in a Chief's Court, which followed Native Law and Custom. They were therefore brought within the exclusive jurisdiction of the European Courts in 1926. (24)

Under British protection and subsidy, the absolutist power of the Chiefs developed as it never could have done, with but few and transient exceptions, prior to the consolidating influence of European rule. It thus became abundantly clear that, if tribalism were to survive, it must perforce submit to some far-reaching measure of control. In Bechuanaland, indeed, 'Indirect Rule' was so 'indirect' as hardly to be 'rule' at all.

In 1922 an attempt was made to interest the Chiefs

and notables in the wider aspects of administration by the creation of a Native Advisory Council, consisting of the Chief and five other representatives of each of the five main tribes. This body meets once a year, and its advice is asked as to the spending of the revenue of the Native Fund. The European Advisory Council, established in 1923, actually meets twice a year, and discusses the estimates at large, even though most of the revenue is contributed by Natives. (25) These bodies are purely advisory, and the Native Council is entirely dominated by absolutist Chiefs.

Draft Proclamations, which aimed at setting up Native Authorities and Native Courts according to a pattern well established in British Tropical Africa, were circulated to the Chiefs in 1933. They were received with considerable opposition, more especially by Acting Chief Tshekedi of the Bamangwato, and something like a deadlock ensued. Into the weary and somewhat sensational details of this Chief's suspension and subsequent reinstatement, it is fortunately unnecessary to enter. The abiding result is likely to be the regulation of tribal powers in a manner guaranteeing respect for traditional authority, while at the same time admitting into tribal organization new forces which alone can make for progress, albeit on Native lines. (26)

12. *Swaziland*

Swaziland is the smallest of the three High Commission Territories. It is also the one in which most land, in proportion to total area, has passed into European ownership, and in which tribal authority has been most closely circumscribed. Its geographical position made it of particular interest to the South African Republic, no less than to Great Britain, and, in the earlier years of European influence, its status was regulated by agreement between these two Powers.

Swaziland is a border territory, somewhat sparsely inhabited by a Bantu people, who are akin to their hereditary foes, the Zulu, and are united, like them, under a Paramount Chief. During the last quarter of the nineteenth century, a certain number of Europeans found their way into this beautiful country, and obtained concessions, mainly for grazing and for minerals, from the ruling Chief. Their advent made Swazi independence—which had been recognized by Great Britain and the South African Republic in 1881—somewhat precarious, and prepared the way for further intervention. After some preliminary uncertainties, Great Britain finally agreed, in 1895, that 'the South African Republic shall have and be secured in all rights and powers of protection, legislation, jurisdiction and administration over Swaziland and the inhabitants thereof', though without actually incorporating it in the territory of the Republic. (27)

The Protectorate exercised by the Republican Government was of short duration, and was proclaimed against the wishes of the Native tribesmen. It ceased to be effective during the Boer War, and when the South African Republic was itself annexed in 1900, its powers over Swaziland passed naturally to Great Britain. With the grant of responsible self-government to the Transvaal, Swaziland was transferred to the High Commissioner for South Africa by an Order in Council of December 1st, 1906, which is the legal basis of the present regime.

One of the first tasks of the new administration was to bring some semblance of order into the tangled mass of concessions, which survived as a painful legacy from the eighteen-eighties and early 'nineties. Grants had then been made wholesale, for different purposes and for varying periods, and with boundaries seldom defined. In the course of time, moreover, many of the claims had been sold, in whole or sometimes only in part. Yet, over these groups 'of conflicting interests, boundaries, and periods there had to be preserved the natural rights of the Natives to live, move, cultivate, graze and hunt'. (28) The Paramount Chiefs of earlier days had received large sums for concessions which, under Native Law and Custom, they were very doubtfully entitled to grant. The money had, of course, been squandered, but the burden of claims remained.

The whole question was carefully examined by a Commission, which reported in 1906. Its recommendations were designed with a view to reserving areas for the exclusive occupation of Natives, adequate not only for their existing needs, but also for future development. It was hoped that this objective would be achieved by reducing the area of all private land concessions by one-third, a principle embodied in the Concessions Partition Proclamation of 1907. (29) This led, two years later, to a final partition, under which the Native Reserves consist of thirty-one separate blocks of land in various parts of the territory. In the selection of these areas every effort was made to avoid the moving of kraals, and to assure to the Natives a fair proportion of the better land. (30) The European concession holders, thanks to their surrender, without compensation, of one-third of the conceded areas, were able, under the Proclamation of 1907, to obtain freehold grants in respect of the remainder. The rest of the country —apart, that is to say, from the Native Reserves and these newly constituted European holdings— was Crown land, which was later disposed of to purchasers under the terms of the Crown Lands Disposal Proclamation of 1911. Another consequence of the partition made in 1909 was that, after the expiry of a period of grace of five years, no Natives were allowed to remain as independent cultivators on land assigned to Europeans.

However fair this settlement of old-time claims

may seem to be, it was certainly not popular amongst
the Natives. Accustomed to stock-raising and to
shifting cultivation, the Swazi resented the very idea
of restriction, which is inherent in any final settlement. In 1914 the then Queen Regent, on her own
initiative, began to buy back alienated land from
Europeans. Her action necessitated the imposition of
special tribal levies, and some of the money thus
raised unfortunately disappeared. This regrettable
affair had as a consequence the formal prohibition
of the sale or lease of land to Natives without the
previous consent of the High Commissioner. (31)
The net result was that, to the Reserves as constituted under the Proclamation of 1907—an area of
approximately 1,633,700 acres—there was added,
at considerable expense, a further 68,500 acres: or a
total of a little over 1,700,000 acres of Native land.
As against this, the area in European occupation
amounts to over 2,400,000 acres, and there is approximately 157,000 acres of Crown land in addition.
It is interesting to notice that the density of population in the Native areas is in the neighbourhood
of 38 to the square mile, while in the European areas
it is only $6\frac{1}{2}$ to the square mile. (32)

This land settlement rankled in the Native mind,
and was challenged in a test case which came before
the Judicial Committee of the Privy Council in
1926. The concession in question had originally
been granted subject to any rights enjoyed by Native
occupiers. As a result of the partition, part of the

land had become a Native Reserve, and the rest the freehold of the concession holder. Their Lordships held that the title of a Native community 'generally takes the form of a usufructuary right, a mere qualification of a burden on the radical or final title of whoever is sovereign'. It followed, therefore, that it could 'be extinguished by the action of a paramount power which assumes possession of the entire control of the land'. (33) The partition was therefore valid and there, from the legal point of view, the matter must be allowed to rest.

The administration was re-organized when the country passed under the control of the High Commissioner in 1906. Its local head is the Resident Commissioner, whose headquarters are now at Mbabane. British Courts were set up to deal with all cases involving Europeans, and with exclusive jurisdiction over Natives in criminal matters. The Swaziland Administration Proclamation of 1907 also defined the judicial powers of the Chiefs, enacting that 'the Paramount Chief and other Native Chiefs shall continue to exercise jurisdiction according to Native Law and Custom in all civil disputes in which Natives only are concerned; provided always that any party to such civil dispute may appeal from the decision of any such Chief to the Court of the Resident Commissioner whose decision shall be final'. (34) This has, at least, the advantage of being perfectly clear, though it seems unfortunate that the Native Courts were not also granted a limited jurisdiction in criminal matters.

Swaziland is a small country which is not over blessed with natural resources. In a certain number of areas, however, the soil is good and the rainfall sufficient for growing dry crops in ordinary years, while tracks of the low veld offer excellent pasturage for cattle. (35) Deposits of gold, alluvial tin, asbestos and coal are known to exist, but their exploitation cannot be said to have been remunerative hitherto. The European community has been sorely tested by the drought of recent years, and, amongst the small farmers in the South of the territory, a real pauper class is in process of formation, whose condition approximates to that of the 'Poor Whites' in the Union. (36)

Native agriculture has been considerably modified by the widespread use of the plough. As in many other parts of Africa, this has unfortunately increased the acreage without necessarily improving the yield of arable land. Moreover, here as elsewhere, the introduction of veterinary services has had the undesired result of encouraging overstocking in the Native areas.

The Native tax was fixed at the basic rate of 40s. for each adult male when the country was administered under the Transvaal, but was reduced to 20s., with a like sum for each wife after the first, up to a maximum of 60s., in 1906. (37) The financial difficulties, which have been a chronic feature of this Protectorate, necessitated an increase to the present rate of 35s. per adult male, while a man with more than one wife pays 30s., and a further 30s. for each wife after the first, up to a maximum of 90s. This is the highest rate of Native taxation in Southern Africa, and would be an intolerable burden but for the flow of Swazi labour to the mines. (38)

Swaziland has never raised sufficient ordinary revenue to meet its expenditure. (39) For close on a quarter of a century, receipts from the sales of Crown land were swallowed up, though this relief has now practically come to an end. Even so, however, the excess of liabilities over assets at the end of the financial year 1932–3 stood at £90,000, which is approximately the total revenue in a normal year: and recourse had already been had to Imperial grants-in-aid. In the financial year 1931–2, out of a total expenditure of £113,000, the administration accounted for $15\frac{1}{2}$ per cent., and police and justice (mainly prisons) for nearly 21 per cent.; as against $12\frac{3}{4}$ per cent. for veterinary and agricultural services, $9\frac{1}{4}$ per cent. for education, and $8\frac{1}{2}$ per cent. for medical services. These percentages compare unfavourably with those for Basutoland, though they look better—on paper—than do the corresponding figures for Bechuanaland. The maintenance of law and order, however, seems very expensive for a territory so small and easy to administer as this.

13. *Some general impressions*

Administrative costs are relatively high in all three territories, though more particularly so in Bechuanaland and Swaziland. This is so, in part, because the Protectorates of Bechuanaland and Swaziland, and the Colony of Basutoland, have been treated, in the main, as separate units, rather than as three provinces of one administration. The consequence has been much triplication, and overhead charges which appear excessive. It would, however, have been difficult to find any other solution, so long as there was doubt as to the future status of these little lands.

The feeling of uncertainty in this respect has also left its mark on the various administrative cadres. The recruiting of the Magistrates has usually been made from the ranks of the police or, as in the Union, from the clerical staff. The former have specialized in Native crime, which is hardly the best preparation for administration of a broader sweep: and neither have, in general, the antecedents and the training now required of our administrators in Tropical Africa. Nor, be it added, are the conditions of service so attractive. The scales of salary are lower; there is little, if any, interchange of officers; and, in consequence, the outlook tends to be parochial.

Judged from the point of view of the British taxpayer, these territories can only be described as a nuisance. Two of them are barely solvent, without intermittent subsidies, and all three of them raise problems, in the economic sphere, which would demand considerable outlay, on capital account, for their solution. Moreover, the economic life of all the three is closely interwoven with that of the Union, in which our own administrations naturally cannot have the very slightest influence.

From the standpoint of the Union, the very existence of a separate administration in these lands is regarded by some people as a challenge to the fitness of South Africa to manage her own affairs. The small White population of the High Commission Territories has little to gain by political exclusion from its natural markets: and, in so far as Swaziland and Bechuanaland are concerned, the progressive pauperization of the smaller men gives them every inducement to look with longing eyes to a land beyond their frontiers with more, and more influential 'Poor Whites'.

Against all this most cogent argument, we have the wishes of close on a million Black men, who are most loyal to the direct connection with Great Britain, which their forebears ardently desired, and who are, rightly or wrongly, exceedingly suspicious of Union Native policy.

Such appear to be the essential facts in this distressing, if diminutive, Imperial problem. As usual, where Natives are concerned, the issue is ultimately one of moral obligation, rather than of what may seem to be a more immediate expediency.

PART III

SOUTHERN RHODESIA

14. *Company rule*

DURING the last quarter of the nineteenth century the Colonial Powers of Europe engaged in a scramble for the African Tropics. The proclamation of a Protectorate over Bechuanaland brought the British flag to the Zambezi, and the activities of the British South Africa Company, which received its Charter in 1889, extended our influence on both banks of that great river. After the rival claims of Portugal had been adjusted, the Company exercised jurisdiction, South of the Zambezi, over a territory of close on 150,000 square miles, separated from the South African Republic by the Limpopo, which received the name of Southern Rhodesia. (1)

The Europeans were late comers to this part of the Continent, where there was land in abundance, and where the Native population was small and scattered. In the uplands of the East a number of separate tribes, conveniently referred to as Mashona, represented an earlier Bantu invasion. They lived in precarious dependence upon their strong and warlike western neighbours, the Amandebele, a people of Zulu stock, who had been driven from the Eastern Transvaal by Boer Voortrekkers in the eighteen-thirties. For over half a century these warriors and pastoralists held sway over Matabeleland, and added to their prowess and their spoils by frequent raids into Mashonaland.

As a result of an agreement signed in 1888, however, Matabeleland became a sphere of British influence, and in the following year the Company received its Charter. By September 1890 the famous band of Pioneers had reached the uplands of Mashonaland and built a fort, to which they gave the name of Salisbury; and then there followed eager search for minerals, and the staking out of European farms.

By the terms of its Charter, the Company was specifically pledged to respect Native rights. Thus 'in the administration of justice to the said peoples or inhabitants, careful regard shall always be had to the customs and laws of the class or tribe or nation to which the parties respectively belong, especially with respect to the holding, possession, transfer and disposition of lands'. (2) The number of European settlers was, however, relatively small, and their arrival did not result in any undue pressure on the land.

The immediate problem in the early 'nineties was the growing restlessness and marked suspicion of the Amandebele to the West of the new settlements. Suffice it here to say that the inevitable clash came in 1893, and resulted in the overthrow of independent Matabeleland. The royal cattle became the property of the conquering Company, and some privately owned beasts shared the same fate. A considerable number of settlers and prospectors were attracted to the country by the lure of gold, and large blocks of land also passed into the hands of exploration companies. This led to considerable pressure upon the local Natives, who were loth to abandon their home districts for the two Reserves set apart for their exclusive use in 1894. Moreover, it seems clear that a certain amount of persuasion was exercised by the administration to procure labour for the various requirements of Government, of mining companies, and private persons. (3) Then came an outbreak of rinderpest, which added to the resentment of a proud people who had not really been subdued, and whose desire for a King of their own was as a 'longing for a fire at which to warm themselves'. The withdrawal of the police, occasioned by the sad adventure of the Jameson raid, afforded the opportunity for a Native rising. This started in Matabeleland in 1896, and soon spread eastward to Mashonaland, challenging the very existence of European rule. Imperial troops helped to put down the insurgents, and, when peace was at last restored, the Company had to submit to a greater measure of Imperial control than had been exercised before.

The position was defined anew by an Order in Council of 1898. (4) The Company remained responsible for the general administration of affairs, and continued to be represented in the country by an Administrator, whom it appointed subject to the approval of the Imperial Government. The Secretary of State, for his part, appointed a Resident Commissioner, who ranked next after the Administrator. He was a member of the Executive and Legislative Councils, and had the right of access to all administrative information. It was the duty of this officer to report to the High Commissioner for South Africa upon every Ordinance and every appointment submitted for approval. (5) He was able to keep the Imperial authorities thoroughly informed on all aspects of the administration, and, more especially, upon the conduct of Native affairs.

The Charter had provided, in general terms, for the administration of the Native peoples, and had aimed, as we have seen, at preserving their rights. The nucleus of an administrative service was formed soon after, and it is interesting to notice that the district officers in these early days were called Collectors, a title not without significance. Under the arrangements made in 1898, however, the organization and status of the service were defined in more detail. The Administrator appointed a Secretary for Native Affairs as the principal executive officer in this department, together with Native Commissioners and Assistant Native Commissioners, who were responsible for administration in the districts. The appointment, dismissal, and remuneration of these officers could only be effected with the approval of the High Commissioner for South Africa, subject to confirmation by the Secretary of State. (6) The members of the Native Department, although appointed and paid by the Company, were thus given very definite safeguards, which were designed to ensure the application of administrative, rather than commercial standards in this all important branch of government.

Native Commissioners were to control the Natives through their tribal Chiefs and Headmen. Subject to the approval of the Administrator in Council, they were, however, given the power, normally vested in the Chief by Native Law, of assigning land to Natives for huts, gardens and grazing grounds in vacant areas, or in the Reserves. The Chiefs were appointed by the Administrator, and were responsible for the good conduct of the people under their charge. They acted, in general, as intermediaries between the Government and the governed, and were required to assist in the registration of huts and the collection of the hut tax, which was first levied at the rate of 10s. a year. In 1901, a poll tax was substituted in its stead, and this was fixed, three years later, at 20s., payable by each adult male, together with an additional tax of 10s. in respect of each wife after the first. (7) It may be noted that the Legislative Council had proposed a tax of 40s., which was disallowed by the Imperial Government. The system of Native taxation, established in 1904, has lasted, with a few minor modifications, down to the present day.

In the judicial sphere, jurisdiction was to be exercised solely by European officers. The principal institutions were the High Court and the Magistrates' Courts, though Native Commissioners were appointed as Special Justices of the Peace, or, if properly qualified, as Magistrates. Natives were given the option of bringing an action either before a Special Justice of the Peace or before a Magistrate, an arrangement which was not calculated to add to the prestige of the Native Department. It was brought to an end when the administration was overhauled in 1910. Thereafter there was a Native Commissioner in each district, who might also be the Magistrate: but, in any case, each Native Commissioner had the jurisdiction of a Magistrate in all civil cases in which Natives only were concerned, and in criminal proceedings in which the accused was a Native. The right of appeal was the same as that from the Court of a Magistrate. (8) This reform made for greater efficiency, by unifying the machinery of administration, and by ensuring that Native cases should be tried by those who knew the Natives best.

The traditional authority of the Chiefs, however, found little place in the administrative system of the Chartered Company. The overthrow of the well-developed tribal order in Matabeleland had been one of the main objects of the War of 1893, and there was never any question of recognizing a successor to Lobengula as Paramount Chief of the Amandebele. The tribal organization of the Mashona was very backward, but the serious rising which took place throughout the country in 1896 made people suspicious of any institution, such as that of the Chieftainship, which, by giving cohesion to Native society, might possibly facilitate rebellion in the future. (9)

The policy of tribal control, as laid down in 1898, was exercised through Chiefs, appointed by the Government, who were normally in the traditional line of tribal succession. They were, however, shorn of much of their power, and their judicial functions were not officially recognized. In actual practice, of course, many matters were still referred to them by the tribesmen for arbitration. So long as these were purely domestic in character, and the Chiefs were not too corrupt, the administration did not interfere, for recourse could always be had to European Courts, should any party so desire. (10) The Native Commissioners doubtless kept, and keep, a watchful eye on all proceedings of the Chiefs, but no recognized system of control over these extra-legal Native Courts has been as yet established.

The Chiefs were regarded as useful adjuncts 'in the investigation of crime, the maintenance of order, and the collection of revenue', (11) but their authority was declining, and it was stated, so long ago as 1909, that, in Mashonaland, at any rate, they had little personal influence with their people apart from the power exercised through the Native Commissioner. (12) It is, therefore, not surprising that the Native Affairs Committee of Enquiry should report, in 1911, that 'contact with civilization has had a retrograde effect, especially in...the lack of respect for parental and tribal authority'. (13) The system of administration was hardly designed to maintain the sanctions of a primitive order of society, though tribal institutions show a remarkable tenacity, and are far from being a negligible factor even now.

The Native rising of 1896 and its aftermath had called attention very forcibly to the need for ensuring adequate reserves of land for the Native population, in view of the encroachments of European prospectors and settlers. The Order in Council of 1898 laid definite obligations upon the administration in this respect by enacting that 'the Company shall from time to time assign to the Natives inhabiting Southern Rhodesia land sufficient for their occupation, whether as tribes or portions of tribes, and suitable for their agricultural and pastoral requirements, including in all cases a fair and equitable proportion of springs or permanent water'. (14) The Native Commissioners were therefore instructed to study the question in their several districts, and to suggest areas which should be set aside for Native occupation. Their proposals were co-ordinated, and finally approved by resolutions of the Executive Council in 1902. (15) Unfortunately, however, the demarcation of these Reserves had not been made in accordance with any definite policy, but had been left to the discretion of the 'men on the spot'. The resultant settlement varied greatly from district to district, and was inevitably prejudiced, in many cases, by an insufficient knowledge of local geography and natural resources. In course of time, moreover, new settlers came into the country, and many Natives, who had hitherto remained on land acquired by Europeans, were given notice to quit, and moved into the nearest Reserves. This resulted in an uneven distribution of the population, with overcrowding in some areas.

We have already seen that the Company was under an obligation to assign, from time to time, sufficient land for Native occupation. As the years went by, it became apparent, on the one hand, that there would ultimately be a geographical limit to the application of such a policy, and, on the other, that the Native population should be given a surer title to its land than that afforded by a resolution of the Executive Council. In view of the importance of the issues involved, and of the certainty of constitutional changes in a relatively near future, a Commission was appointed in 1915, under an agreement reached between the Imperial Government and the Chartered Company, to investigate the

whole question of Native Reserves in Southern
Rhodesia. (16)

The Commissioners refused to admit that the
Native had an 'indefeasible right to land sufficient
for his occupation and suitable for his agricultural
and pastoral requirements according to the primitive methods of Native life', since this would ultimately mean that the whole country would pass into
his hands. (17) A detailed study of the situation led
them to suggest certain modifications in the existing
settlement. These involved a re-grouping of some
of the Reserves, in order to establish a clearer demarcation between European and Native lands, and
also a small reduction in the total area. The result
they regarded as adequate for existing needs, and
also for the probable requirements of an expanding
population in the future.

Their findings were embodied, with some modifications, in the Southern Rhodesia Order in Council
of 1920. The Reserves then established were 'vested
in the High Commissioner, and set apart for the sole
and exclusive use and occupation of the Native
inhabitants of Southern Rhodesia'. Out of a total
area of 96 million acres, these Reserves amount to
something over $21\frac{1}{2}$ million acres, or close on $22\frac{1}{2}$ per
cent. of the country. The acreage allotted to Natives
in Southern Rhodesia is thus approximately the
same as that included in the Native Reserves in the
Union of South Africa, though the total Native
population only amounts to about a million, as

against some 5½ millions. The historical antecedents of the problem have, of course, been utterly different in the two countries, and the adequacy of a land settlement cannot be measured by a mere count of the acres involved. When all is said, however, the arrangement adopted in 1920 ensured that tribal society in Southern Rhodesia should at least have room to live.

While the first steps were thus being taken towards a solution of the question of the land, certain minor adjustments were made in the administrative machine. Up to 1910, the Secretary for Native Affairs had been the principal administrative officer in the department. In that year the Administrator was empowered to exercise these functions himself though, if he did so, a special Assistant was to be appointed. Provision was also made for the appointment of Superintendents of Natives in important areas. (18) A further change came, in 1913, with the appointment of one Chief Native Commissioner for the whole country, instead of one for each Province as heretofore. (19)

Native administration under the Company aimed at justice and impartiality, rather than at anything approaching innovation. On the one hand, the Imperial Government guaranteed equality of treatment in the Order in Council of 1898, which

stipulates that 'no conditions, disabilities or restrictions shall, without the previous consent of a
Secretary of State, be imposed upon Natives by
Ordinance which do not equally apply to persons of
European descent, save in respect of the supply of
arms, ammunition and liquor'. [20] Natives were
also able to acquire or dispose of land, subject to
certain conditions designed for their own protection,
though, in actual practice, they hardly ever did
so. [21] On the other hand, tribal authority was being
steadily undermined, and virtually nothing was being
put in its place. Missionaries were busy in Southern
Rhodesia as in other parts of Africa, but educational
activities received little financial assistance from a
Government whose administrative budget regularly
showed a balance on the wrong side.

The primary aim of the Chartered Company was,
of course, the exploitation of the economic resources
of the country. With this end in view, it did everything in its power to encourage European settlement, a policy which relegated Native development
to a secondary place. In course of time, however,
the European population claimed an ever greater
voice in the affairs of government. After long nego-
tiations with the Imperial authorities, and legal
process, relating primarily to claims for compensation, which do not directly concern us here, the
period of Company rule came to an end. A refer-
endum held in 1922 showed that a majority of White
Rhodesians favoured responsible self-government,

rather than union with South Africa, and, in the following year, the territory became a self-governing Colony. (22) Subject to certain safeguards maintained, above all, in the interest of an overwhelming majority of Natives, the government of Southern Rhodesia passed from the Chartered Company to the local European inhabitants, who numbered, at that time, some thirty-four thousand.

15. *Native policy since* 1923

Company rule lasted for over a generation, and, during that period, an administrative tradition grew up in the field of Native policy which has continued, with certain minor modifications, through the first decade of responsible self-government. Moreover, the control hitherto exercised by the Imperial Authorities in Native affairs was in large measure maintained in the new Constitution, and the Southern Rhodesia Legislature is precluded from passing any laws concerning three matters which are declared to be reserved subjects by the Letters Patent of 1923. (23) One of these is the salary of the Governor, who is the local representative of His Majesty the King. The others are of more immediate importance for our present purpose.

The Governor is instructed to reserve any bills dealing with certain specified matters for His Majesty's pleasure, and this power of reservation cannot be altered by any Act of the Colonial Legislature. It will suffice here to say that the Governor shall reserve 'any Law, save in respect of the supply of arms, ammunition or liquor to Natives, whereby Natives may be subjected or made liable to any conditions, disabilities or restrictions to which persons of European descent are not also subjected or made liable'. (24)

The sections dealing with Native administration form the remaining category of reserved subjects. The permanent head of the Native Department, who, under the new regime, will be the Chief Native Commissioner, is appointed by the Governor in Council, subject to the approval of the High Commissioner for South Africa. The subordinate officials of the Department are appointed in the same way, and their salaries are similarly safeguarded. These officers may be removed by the Governor-in-Council, with the approval of the High Commissioner, but not otherwise. (25)

The land settlement was specifically included in this group of reserved subjects. 'The Southern Rhodesia Order in Council, 1920, whereby the lands known as the Native Reserves were vested in the High Commissioner and set apart for the sole and exclusive use of the Native inhabitants of Southern Rhodesia, shall continue in full force and effect as if it formed part of these Our Letters Patent, and no portion of the land comprised within the said Reserves shall be alienated except for the purposes authorized by the said Order, and then only in exchange for other suitable land.' (26)

Another of the former guarantees incorporated in the Letters Patent of 1923 was that which enabled Natives to acquire or dispose of land on the same conditions as non-Natives, provided that no contract for encumbering or alienating land the property of a Native should be valid unless made in the presence of a Magistrate, who states that the consideration is fair and reasonable, and that the Native understands the transaction. (27)

This guarantee to Natives of the right to acquire land in any part of the country had been opposed by the delegation of elected members of the old Legislative Council, who visited London in 1921 to discuss the drafting of a provisional scheme of self-government for Southern Rhodesia. They had suggested, as an alternative, that specific districts should be set aside by the High Commissioner in which Natives only might acquire land, and within which Europeans should not be allowed to do so. The Secretary of State declared himself unwilling to accept a policy which would presumably imply, as a corollary, the exclusion of Natives from other areas. He promised, however, that if a full and impartial enquiry should show, after responsible government had come into force, that some amendment of the law were necessary, the British Government would be prepared to consider the matter anew.

This was the origin of the Land Commission of 1925, which was appointed to report on the expe-

diency of setting apart defined areas, outside the
Native Reserves, within which (a) Natives only, and
(b) Europeans only, should be permitted to acquire
land. Should the Committee consider such a policy
to be desirable, it was to make recommendations as
to how it could best be achieved. (28)

On the major question of principle, the Commission found virtually unanimous support, amongst
all classes of the inhabitants, for the view that the
points of contact between Europeans and Natives
should be reduced to a minimum. They therefore
advocated a policy of 'possessory segregation'—
the separation of the races so far as landholding is
concerned—and recommended that separate areas
should be set aside, for Europeans and for Natives,
in all parts of the country where applications for
land were being made, or were likely to be made in
the near future. So far as possible, existing European interests should be left undisturbed, and
further acquisitions allowed in what were already
predominantly White areas. Similar considerations should apply in the allocation of land for
purchase by Natives, and the areas demarcated for
that purpose should adjoin the Reserves wherever
possible.

Landholding in the Reserves is essentially communal in character, and it is doubtful whether individual tenure would be possible under existing
legislation. The Commission considered that, as
things were, it would be premature to make the

introduction of individual holdings even permissive in the majority of the Reserves. The principal object, therefore, was to provide land outside the Reserves for private occupation by Natives, and, more especially, by those living on unalienated Crown land, and in private locations under agreement to pay rent. (29)

Natives in European areas may be divided into three main categories, according to whether they live on privately owned land, on unalienated Crown land, or in or near the towns. Those on private farms, again, live there either under labour agreements, or as rent-paying tenants. Before the War the latter class had been growing in numbers, and the rent demanded from them had risen steadily. It varied from 10s. to 40s. for each male adult, while an extra charge was sometimes made for polygamous wives. (30) The authorities had no wish to encourage the growth of a European landlord class, and a considerable measure of control was established over private locations in 1910. Thereafter Natives, other than labourers, were only allowed to reside on European land if a written agreement with the landholder had been entered into in the presence of the Native Commissioner of the district, attested by him, if he were satisfied that its terms were fully understood and accepted by the Native, and approved by the Chief Native Commissioner. (31) In the interest of all parties, the Commission of 1925 recommended that Natives should, as a general rule, no longer be permitted to reside as rent-paying tenants on European farms. (32)

Natives settled on unalienated Crown land live, for the most part, in tribal communities, and pay an annual rental. The Commissioners thought that these people should be encouraged to move into specifically Native areas, and that no further permits should be granted to newcomers, though they considered that those already established might well be allowed to remain until the land was actually alienated.

Urban development is as yet in its infancy, and there is still time to prevent the emergence, in Rhodesia, of a complex of problems which has become well-nigh insoluble in the Union. It should be remembered, however, that the 'Native population is present in the towns not only in its own interests in order to earn a living, but in the interests of the White population which, under the existing system, is dependent on Native labour'. (33)

Natives were legally entitled to acquire land in any part of a municipal area on the same terms as Europeans, though they doubtless did not do so in practice. Adopting once again the principle of possessory segregation, the Commission recommended that the right of purchase in urban areas should be restricted in the future to Native Locations, where special sites should be set aside for better-class Native dwellings. Moreover, village settlements should also be established in the neighbourhood of the principal towns, so that plots might be available for cultivation by the women. This provision was intended to bridge over the difficult transition from rural to urban conditions.

With certain relatively minor exceptions, the recommendations of the Commission were embodied in a measure which required the approval of the British Government, in so far as it concerned one of the 'reserved subjects'. This was given in due course, and the bill became law under the title of the Land Apportionment Act of 1930.

The land of Southern Rhodesia, outside the Native Reserves, is henceforward divided into five categories, of which the Forest Area does not call for more than passing mention here. In those parts of the country which are to form the European Area, no Native shall, in future, be allowed to hold or occupy land, and existing Native claims, though safeguarded, are liable to expropriation. This does not, however, necessarily apply to Crown Land, where the conditions of Native occupation may be prescribed from time to time. No agreement, made by a Native, to occupy land on payment of rent to the European owner is to run for more than six years after the Act comes into force, though a Native may still occupy alienated land in return for labour service to the owner, on terms to be approved by the Chief Native Commissioner. (34) On the other hand, in the zone which is scheduled as coming within the Native Area, no person other than a Native shall

hold or occupy land, save under the terms of the
Mining Laws, and any existing rights of non-Natives
shall be liable to expropriation. In this area, land
may be granted to indigenous Natives, subject to
such conditions as may be prescribed by the Land
Board, a body composed of the Chief Native Commissioner, as Chairman, together with not less than
four other members, of whom one must be nominated
by the High Commissioner, and of whom none may
be a member of the Colonial Legislature. No land
acquired in this zone can be alienated or in any way
encumbered without the prior consent of the Land
Board. (35)

In addition to the two principal categories of
what are ultimately intended to become exclusively
European and exclusively Native Areas of ownership, certain lands, consisting for the most part of
European farms which form an entrant angle in
scheduled Native Areas, are classified as 'Unde-
termined'. In this zone Native holdings cannot be
sold to non-Natives, though European holdings
may be disposed of freely, provided always that if
any such land be acquired by a Native, it will be
subject to the same conditions as land in a Native
Area. (36)

Considerable tracts of country which are unlikely
to be the subject of applications in the more immediate future, are described as the Unassigned
Area. The Governor-in-Council is empowered to include any portion of this either in the European or

in the Native Area, but, until such action is taken, no alienation is permitted, and the granting of leases is limited, both as to time and space. Unless so alienated or granted under lease, all land in this zone is to remain available for Native occupation. (37)

The Act thus lays down a comprehensive programme for the future assignment of land as between the two races, and yet leaves a margin for contingencies which cannot now be foreseen. The areas involved are summarized below.

	Million acres
Native Reserves	21·6
Native Area	7·5
Undetermined Area	0·1
Forest Area	0·6
Unassigned Area	17·8
European Area	48·7
Total	96·3

It will be seen that a little over one-half of the total area of the country is set aside for ownership by Europeans, while the Native Reserves account for some 22½ per cent., and the new Native Area, which is commonly referred to as the Native Purchase Area, amounts to a further 7¾ per cent. Approximately 18½ per cent. still awaits final adjudication.

Some light is thrown on the land settlement by a consideration of the approximate movement and distribution of the Native population of recent years.

Native population	(In thousands)		
	1924	1928	1932
In Reserves	508·3	587·7	656·9
On Unalienated Land	128·7	130·0	161·7
On Alienated Land	150·4	179·5	182·3
In Mines and Towns	25·2	22·6	8·3
Total	812·6	919·8	1009·2

These figures are far from accurate. (38) In the case of the urban population they are only meant to include those permanently settled in the towns, and the method of enumeration seems to have changed. Even so, the general picture they present is probably fairly correct. Some two-thirds of the Natives live in the Reserves: the rural population is increasing most rapidly, of recent years, on Unalienated (Crown) Land, and very little on land alienated to Europeans: while the permanent town dwellers form a negligible fraction of the total.

The Southern Rhodesian Native is essentially an agriculturist and pastoralist, who does not normally take kindly to work in the mines. The existence of adequate supplies of land, moreover, relieves him from the pressure to seek work away from his home which is so marked a feature of Native life in the Union. These facts will help to explain the figures of local and alien Native labour engaged in the mining industry before and after the War.

Native Labourers in the Mines

	1910	1930
Local	12,739	11,644
Alien	25,086	33,698
Total	37,825	45,342

The dependence upon outside supplies of labour is, indeed, one of the most characteristic features of the industry, and both Nyasaland and Northern Rhodesia normally provide more Native workers for the mines than does Southern Rhodesia itself.

Some of these immigrants from other territories, who are, of course, entirely removed from tribal control, remain for long periods in the Colony, and more especially in the towns. It seems probable, moreover, that a growing number of local Natives will, in course of time, engage in industrial pursuits, (39) and they too will presumably seek to establish themselves in or near the towns. The Government, therefore, very wisely followed the recommendations of the Land Commission by taking power, in the Land Apportionment Act of 1930, to set up Village Settlements in the neighbourhood of towns. (40) The first experiments in this direction mark an interesting departure in Native Policy in urban areas.

The rural Natives make up some 99 per cent. of
the total population, and, for the most part, still live
a tribal life, based on a communal system of land
tenure. The institution of the Chieftainship has certainly suffered something of an eclipse during the
forty years or so of British rule, but it nevertheless
remains the pivot of Native society. This fact does
not seem to have received official recognition as yet,
and its importance is hardly apparent in recent administrative reports.[41]

It will be remembered that the Union Native
Administration Act of 1927 proposed to strengthen
tribal authority in South Africa by permitting the
grant of judicial powers to Chiefs in civil cases, and
that the policy of development along tribal lines was
heartily endorsed by the Native Economic Commission appointed by the Union Government in
1930. Of this new outlook, which also characterizes
Native policy in most parts of Tropical Africa, there
was, however, no trace in the Southern Rhodesia
Native Affairs Act of 1927, a consolidating measure
which, with minor amendments, is the basic statute
governing Native administration in the Colony.[42]
Another Act of the same year, however, abolished
trial by jury, and enacted in its place that any Native
coming before the High Court should be tried by
a Judge sitting with two special Assessors who must
be, or must have been, Native Commissioners.[43] The
substitution of two men well versed in Native habits
for twelve citizens who might be influenced by lack

of knowledge of the Native outlook, or even, wittingly or unwittingly, by a certain measure of prejudice against the Black man, was certainly a step in the right direction.

Until quite recently the trend of Native policy in Southern Rhodesia has followed, in the main, that of the territories now united in the Union of South Africa, with, of course, the one outstanding difference of the question of the land. The dominant influence of the Southern example was doubtless responsible for the reference to the Council system in the Letters Patent of 1923. It was there declared to be 'lawful for the Governor-in-Council, subject to the approval of the High Commissioner, to establish by Proclamation in any Native Reserve or Reserves such Council or Councils of indigenous Natives representative of the local Chiefs and other Native residents... for the discussion... of any matters upon which, as being of direct interest or concern to the Native population generally or to any portion thereof, he may desire to ascertain, or they may desire to submit their views'. (44)

For several years no effort was made to translate this provision into actual practice, and contact was maintained between the Native Commissioners and local Native opinion by the holding of annual meetings in the districts. It was believed that the Rhodesian Natives were not as yet ready for Councils fully-fledged on the Transkeian model, though a first step was taken, in 1930, when informal Native Boards were established. These began to function in the following year, and took the place of the customary district meetings. They meet under the Chairmanship of the local Native Commissioner, and are composed of the subsidized Chiefs and Headmen, *ex officio*, together with an equal number of elected members.

The working of these Boards is in the earliest stages of experiment, but the delay in implementing the intentions of the Constitution is almost certainly a blessing in disguise. Much has happened in Africa since 1923, and from the accumulation of experience elsewhere, Southern Rhodesia is now well placed to profit. The European population, of some 50,000, occupies the geographic backbone of the country, and is outnumbered by the Native by twenty to one. It is, however, possible for European and Native to live side by side in peace: the terms of the Land Apportionment Act of 1930 leave room enough for both. The problem, therefore, is, in essence, whether the Abantu as a whole are to develop in accordance with their own traditions, or whether they are to become rapidly detribalized. The fate of both races in the country must clearly depend upon the answer which this question will receive.

Southern Rhodesia is, of all lands, that in which to strengthen and reform indigenous society, so far as possible on Native lines, should surely be a

major objective of Government policy. The Council
system is a foreign expedient. In the Union, its
success has really been confined to its first home
in the Transkei, and even there, apart from Fingoland, the tribal element is now receiving more
attention than ever before. Its further development
in Southern Rhodesia may therefore well be allowed
to wait until Bantu tribalism has received a greater
measure of recognition and control.

Native administration is not merely concerned
with primitive life as it finds it: it must also have
regard to the factor of change, inevitable when
backward peoples are rushed into contact with an
acquisitive society. Its aim is thus a fusion of progress and stability—an aspect of the problem which,
in Southern Rhodesia, did not at once receive the
attention it merits.

The London Missionary Society began operations
in Matabeleland in 1859, and, as the years went by,
a number of other organizations extended their
activities North of the Limpopo. An Education
Ordinance, passed in 1899, recognized the principle
of Government grants to approved educational
establishments, and, four years later, Native schools
were graded with this object in view. Although the
importance of education for the well-being and advancement of the Native population was gaining
recognition, the financial assistance given by the

Government long remained on a very modest scale. In 1908, for example, the total grants earned by State-aided schools only amounted to £1192. Two years later provision was made for European instructors in agriculture and industrial work, and, in 1920 and 1921, two important Government schools were established, with special sections for the training of Native agricultural demonstrators.

Attention was focussed on the importance of Native development by the Report of a Commission on Native Education, which was published in 1925. (45) For close on a generation this matter had been entrusted to the Department of Education, which was principally concerned with the needs of the European population. The creation of a separate Department of Native Education, in 1928, was, therefore, in itself a sign of new interest. This was followed by the passing of the Native Development Act of 1929, which centralized in one Department all Government activities connected with 'the education of Natives and any other work primarily designed to further the agricultural, industrial, physical or social advancement of Natives'. (46) Education is no longer to be restricted to the somewhat narrow limits of the school: it is to embrace community activities as well. Agricultural training is clearly educational in scope, and the Department which trains Native Demonstrators will henceforward employ them on work in the Reserves. (47) Moreover, in one or two districts, the Natives have

already been persuaded to make a permanent separation of the arable from the grazing lands. By thus
centralizing the arable, rotation of crops and other
improvements can be introduced, and the system
of Native landholding will be gradually trans-
formed. These experiments are taking place in close
proximity to the schools, with great advantage to
all concerned.

Native welfare work is being encouraged by the
training of men and women ('village guides') on
what is usually, if somewhat erroneously, called the
Jeanes method. Two courses were started in 1929,
and although the experiment is not perhaps so im-
pressive, in simplicity and effectiveness, as that at
the Jeanes School near Zomba in Nyasaland, such
an approach to one of the major problems of Native
development offers considerable promise for the
future.(48) In this, as in its other educational activities, it is the policy of the Department to work in
the closest collaboration with the various missionary
bodies.

From the administrative point of view, it is not
easy to define the precise relationship existing between the new Department of Native Development
and the old-established Native Department. There
is clearly a danger, under certain circumstances, of
inter-departmental friction, for administration and
development are most closely bound up together.
Unfortunately, moreover, the Department of Native
Development was placed under the Colonial Secre-

tary, while that of Native Affairs has always been under the Prime Minister. This division lasted down to the autumn of 1933, but the Prime Minister then assumed direct responsibility for both Departments, a more logical arrangement which should simplify the situation in the future.

The most serious obstacle to Native development is the shortage of funds. Expenditure has certainly increased rapidly under responsible government, and the vote on Native education rose from £34,269 in 1925–6 to £69,864 in 1929–30. Even this latter figure, however, is relatively small, both in relation to the needs of the case, and when compared with equivalent expenditure in other parts of Southern Africa. An exact comparison is, of course, impossible, but the relationship between the yield of the Native tax and expenditure on Native education affords a rough guide. In the year 1929–30, the figures were as follows in the Union of South Africa and in Southern Rhodesia respectively. (49)

1929–30	(1) Revenue from Native tax	(2) Expenditure on Native education	(2) as percent. of (1)
	£	£	
Union of South Africa	993,600	570,581	57·4
Southern Rhodesia	343,688	69,864	20·3

On an approximate *per caput* basis, the Union Native, in the year 1929–30, paid something in the neighbourhood of 3s. 9d. in general tax—the local tax is additional, but the proceeds are earmarked for expenditure in the Reserves—while the Southern Rhodesian Native paid about 7s. 3d. in Native tax. Expenditure on Native education in that year was about 2s. 2d. a head in the Union, as against 1s. 6d. in Southern Rhodesia.

The future of Southern Rhodesia clearly depends upon harmonious co-operation between the various peoples within its frontiers. In the economic sphere, the development of the Native as a producer of primary products would add to the wealth of the community as a whole, and would greatly increase the local market for the products of the secondary industries which are already springing up in the country. The employment of Natives in industry produces the same result, and also gives rise to an increased demand for skilled European supervision. (50) Any programme of Native development should, therefore, be based upon the possibilities of the Native population, both as producers and consumers, and expenditure on such a programme is a wise investment. (51)

Southern Rhodesia is in many ways a fortunate country. The settlement of the land question was conceived on broad and statesmanlike lines, and urban development is being controlled while there is still time. With more attention to the administrative possibilities inherent in tribal society, and with increased expenditure on Native development, it would probably be the best placed of all 'mixed States' to solve the many problems which must needs arise when contact is established between an advanced and a more primitive society.

PART IV

SOUTH WEST AFRICA

16. *German colonization*

IN the early eighteen-eighties the European Powers began to show a new interest in Africa, and not the least significant feature of the period was the advent of the Germany of Bismarck to the colonial scene. She looked around, even in the most unlikely directions, to find a place in the sun before it was too late.

The stretch of some eight hundred and fifty miles of coast between the Cunene River, which is the southern frontier of Portuguese Angola, and the Orange River, remained a No-Man's land but for the port of Walvis Bay, which was occupied by Great Britain in 1878. Five years later, however, Lüderitz, a German business man, established a small settlement on this coast, and thereupon Bismarck asked the British Government if it asserted any prior claim. The answer was delayed and, tired of long waiting, Germany proclaimed a Protectorate over the whole of South West Africa, with the exception of Walvis Bay, in 1884. This was recognized by Great Britain in due course. There really was no alternative, since, as Lord Derby wrote, we 'could not fairly grudge to a friendly Power a country

difficult of development, with regard to which it
might have been said that we had never thought
it worth while acquiring until it seemed to be wanted
by our neighbour'.

The Protectorate of South West Africa, as finally
delimited, is a vast territory of over 322,000 square
miles, though much of it is arid and only very
sparsely peopled. Separated from the sea by a rain-
less desert, the core of the country is a large plateau,
interspersed with mountain ranges, which reaches
its greatest average elevation in the neighbourhood
of Windhoek, chosen by the Germans as their
capital. From next to nothing in the coastal belt
the rainfall rises steadily as one proceeds from the
South and West through the central highlands to
the North East. Vegetation follows the same
general direction, from sandy desert through barren
steppe to bush and grassland North and West of
Windhoek, until finally one reaches the tropical
forests of the Okavango and the Zambezi. From the
health point of view, the coast and central highlands
can be regarded as suitable for European settlement, while in the North and East the tropical
climate makes this impossible.

In German days the upland areas of the Centre
and the South were brought under European administration, and included in what was called the
'Police Zone'. Here the Native population was
scanty, and European settlement was actively encouraged. In the process singularly little attention

was paid to Native claims to land, and this German essay in colonization became a fight for very existence between the European cattle farmers and the motley array of peoples upon whom they depended for their labour supply. The little group of Bastards —a cross of Hottentot and Boer—who had migrated from the Cape to the Rehoboth district in 1871, were guaranteed their local rights under treaty. But they were an exception. The vast majority of Natives, including the Hottentots proper, and the Herero, a Bantu-speaking people who had come down from the North, were soon driven to desperation by the exactions of their new masters; while the most primitive relics of them all, the Bushmen, could expect little attention from the colonists. They were allowed to live, so long as they did no damage, but if they failed to fulfil this condition, they were shot down like wild beasts. (1)

In 1903 the Bondelzwarts, a tiny Hottentot people with some slight admixture of European blood, rose in revolt, and were followed in the next year by the much more numerous Herero. This was to be a war almost of extermination for, though the Herero suffered a serious reverse in August 1904, a general rising of the Hottentots took place in the following October, and guerilla warfare dragged out its cruel course till the end of 1906. Indeed, the so-called Simon Copper Hottentots were not defeated until March 1908, when the remnants of the tribe fled across the border to settle in Bechuanaland.

This bare chronicle will give some rough idea of the extent to which German rule was detested by the tribes. When the rising was over the pastoralist Herero, whose numbers had been sadly reduced, were left as landless paupers, and were even prohibited by government from owning cattle. Their lot was to be that of hewers of wood and drawers of water for their European conquerors. There were a few Reserves, chiefly for the Berseba Hottentots, the Bondelzwarts and the Bergdamara, which had been recognized by treaty, but the total area was small and the population insignificant. In the Police Zone as a whole a sullen mass of Natives was 'encouraged' to work for German masters. With the exception of certain Captains of the Berseba and the Bastards, who exercised jurisdiction over their own people, administration was entirely in the hands of German District Officers who did, however, apply Native Law and Custom in civil cases where Natives only were concerned. There was no Native tax for the territory as a whole, though it was introduced in some districts, and varied according to the monthly wage. (2)

Outside the Police Zone the country was not really under administration at all, and no German officials seem to have been stationed amongst the tribes of the North and North East. The Ovambo might appear as a potential source of Black labour for the future, but as their country was quite unsuitable for European settlement, it was their good fortune to live in a much freer relationship to the Protecting Power than the wretched Herero and Hottentots.

Such in brief outline, had been the administration of the territory which was occupied by South African troops in 1915. The Natives, and especially the Herero, welcomed the change, and not unnaturally refused to work for their defeated German masters, of whom many still remained in the country. This threatened serious economic dislocation, and, in an official report, we read that 'it was only by the exercise of a large amount of tact and patience and forceful persuasion that the military administration was then able to maintain a supply of labour'. (3) But the prohibition of stock-owning by Natives was repealed, and a tentative beginning was made with the delimitation of additional Reserves for Native occupation.

The territory remained under martial law from the conquest in 1915 to October 1920. It was ceded by Germany to the Principal Allied and Associated Powers under Article 119 of the Treaty of Versailles, and was assigned by the Supreme Council of the Allies, in May 1919, to His Britannic Majesty, to be administered on His behalf by the Government of the Union of South Africa, under a Mandate to be approved by the Council of the League of Nations. The terms of the Mandate were in accord with Article 22 of the Covenant of the League, which states that to those 'peoples not yet able to stand

by themselves under the strenuous conditions of
the modern world, there should be applied the
principle that the well-being and development of
such peoples form a sacred trust of civilization'.

17. *Administration under mandate*

The Mandate for South West Africa is a so-called
C Mandate, and gives the Mandatory wider powers
than those conferred by the A Mandates, which
apply to territories formerly forming part of the
Turkish Empire, or by the B Mandates, granted in
respect of certain territories in Central Africa. Its
terms were approved by the Council of the League
on December 17th, 1920, and form the basis of the
constitution.

The Union is empowered to administer South
West Africa as an integral portion of its own territory, and may apply to it its own laws, subject to
such local modifications as circumstances may require. It undertakes, however, to 'promote to the
utmost the material and moral well-being and the
social progress of the inhabitants of the territory'
(Article 2). The slave trade is prohibited, and no
forced labour shall be permitted except for essential
public works and services, and then only for adequate remuneration. The strictest control is to be
exercised over the traffic in arms and ammunition,
while the sale to Natives of intoxicating spirits and
beverages is prohibited (Article 3). The military

training of the Natives is to be limited to purposes of internal police and local defence (Article 4). The Mandatory guarantees the free exercise of all forms of worship, and will accord to missionaries, who are nationals of any Member of the League, the right to carry on their calling within the territory (Article 5). An annual report must be presented to the Council of the League, and this will be examined by the Permanent Mandates Commission, a body which acts for the Council in an advisory capacity.

In South West Africa the Government is thus under a formal obligation to carry out its work in accordance with the principle of trusteeship: and the very fact of an annual report to an international body brings the territory into the full light of world publicity. Yet Native policy is not a simple matter. A strong bias of unenlightenment survives from earlier days, and the Natives were sadly disappointed that their country was not restored to them, and the Germans driven out, after the War. (4) Nor is the Native question made any easier by regarding it as synonymous with the labour question, as was once the fashion. (5) Moreover, in the Police Zone, tribal organization has almost entirely disappeared and, in any case, the Native population is not only very small, but is also divided amongst a motley congeries of peoples. The country is both large and poor and, under such conditions, administration is bound to be a costly business. The task of the Union Government is, therefore, not an enviable one and, as the years roll on, it has been complicated by the growth of an aggressive nationalism amongst the Germans, which threatens to make the European question almost as difficult as the Native.

Under the constitution established in 1925, the European inhabitants have the right to elect members to the Legislative Assembly, but this body is not competent to deal with 'Native affairs or any matters specially affecting Natives, including the imposition of taxation upon the persons, land, habitations or earnings of Natives'. (6) All such questions are reserved to the Administrator in Advisory Council. This Council consists of eight members, of whom one must be an 'official who shall be selected mainly on the ground of his thorough acquaintance ...with the reasonable wants and wishes of the non-European races in the territory'. (7)

The territory of South West Africa includes a narrow corridor of land in the extreme North East which gives access to the Zambezi. This is known as the Caprivi Zipfel, after the Chancellor who negotiated its transfer to the German Crown in 1890. On account of its remoteness from the rest of the territory, the Union Government arranged that the Caprivi Strip should be administered by the Bechuanaland Protectorate authorities as from 1921. This solution received a certain amount of criticism at Geneva on formal grounds, and the administration was, therefore, resumed by the Union in September, 1929.

The total Native population of a country which, as we have seen, has an area of 322,000 square miles —six times that of England and Wales, and slightly larger than the Cape Province and Natal combined —is under a quarter of a million, as compared with a European population of some thirty thousand. (8) Its approximate distribution in 1932 was as follows:

Native Population, 1932

Within the Police Zone		89,046
Outside the Police Zone:		
Ovamboland	117,000	
Kaokoveld	4,669	
Okavango	20,566	
Caprivi Zipfel	11,009	153,244
	Total	242,290

The distinction between the Police Zone—which represents the limits of effective occupation in German days, and includes practically the whole of the European population—and the territories outside is of the greatest importance. In the Police Zone, tribalism has completely broken down, and the Natives are in close contact with Europeans. In Ovamboland, on the other hand, tribal organization is strong, and agriculture provides a settled basis for Native life. Almost everywhere else in the territory, the Natives are pastoralists pure and simple.

The main tasks of the Union authorities hitherto have been to settle the land question inside the

Police Zone by the creation of Reserves; to arrange for the organization of Native administration in these Reserves, and also amongst Natives living on European-owned land and in the towns; and to bring the Natives outside the Police Zone under closer administration.

A Native Affairs branch was set up under a Native Commissioner for the whole territory. In general, however, Magistrates exercise jurisdiction over Europeans and Natives alike in the Police Zone, though special officers are appointed for the principal urban centres, such as Windhoek and Lüderitz, together with Superintendents, responsible to the District Magistrates, in the larger Reserves. Headmen, elected by the people, form the link between Government and the Natives living in the Reserves. They take the place of the former Chiefs and arbitrate unofficially in civil disputes. This general pattern is familiar enough to students of Native policy in Southern Africa, and shows no signs of originality. In fact, apart from an important provision for the establishment of Native Reserves, the Native Administration Proclamation of 1922 was primarily concerned with controlling the movements of Natives and with the institution of pass regulations, which do not, however, apply to the purely Native areas outside the Police Zone.

In German days approximately 2,487,000 acres of land had been set aside as Native Reserves. To this a further area of some 4,952,000 acres was added under the powers conferred by the Proclamation of 1922. (9) In considering these figures it should be remembered that the central uplands are an arid region, and that much remains to be done to ensure water supplies adequate even for primitive stock-raising. We are here concerned only with the country included in the Police Zone, and the relative importance of the Reserves will be apparent from the estimated distribution of Native population in 1932.

Native Population in the Police Zone, 1932

	Total	Of which men form	
		Total	Percent.
In Native Reserves	19,464	5,290	27·2
In Urban Areas	19,683	7,036	35·7
In Rural Areas	49,899	17,204	34·5
Total	89,046	29,530	33·2

Less than a quarter of the Native population of the Police Zone lives in the Reserves, and the low percentage of adult males residing there suggests that these are essentially reserves of Native labour. This would seem to be in accordance with official policy. In the annual report for 1928 it is stated that 'men are not encouraged to remain idling in the Reserves. Only men who are physically unfit, or such as are necessarily required to look after the people in the Reserves and their stock and the stock of others who have gone out to seek work, are encouraged to remain there'. (10)

In South West Africa there is no specific direct tax payable by Natives such, for example, as the general tax levied in the Union. They are nominally liable to the same direct taxes as Europeans, but this obligation is virtually limited to the dog tax, now levied at 10*s*. a year. Natives living in the Reserves and on Crown lands outside the Reserves, however, pay grazing fees for the use of the land. In 1924, power was taken to establish Trust Funds in each Native Reserve constituted under the Proclamation of 1922, and these receive such of the revenues raised locally as the Administrator may from time to time determine. (11) In practice they are credited with the receipts from grazing fees, dog tax, and rentals of trading sites, but the total is not very imposing, and only amounts to some £7000 a year for all Reserve Trust Funds combined. This money may be expended on scholastic, agricultural or industrial instruction or demonstration: on improving live-stock: on water supplies: or on general utilities, such as roads and hospitals. Up to the present, the funds available have been utilized solely for development work. On the analogy of the Council System in the Union, a Board is set up in each Reserve, consisting of the local European officer, the Headman, and not more than six persons elected by the people: while a general meeting of all the residents of the Reserves is held annually.

In view of the large proportion of Natives living in rural areas outside the Reserves, it would hardly seem as though the present land settlement, improvement though it is on that of German days, were either generous or adequate. But more serious still is the state of stagnation prevailing in the Reserves themselves. The principal limiting factor is, of course, the acute shortage of water, and it is not easy to see how this can be remedied in so poor a country as South West Africa. It will clearly not be possible for the Reserves to meet the capital charges involved in any important development scheme out of their own meagre resources.

In the urban areas, Native policy follows the familiar Union pattern. In fact, the general provisions of the Natives (Urban Areas) Act of 1923 were applied to South West Africa, with such omissions as were necessary, in 1924. (12)

The Native population of the Police Zone makes up in variety what it lacks in numbers. The estimates for 1932 present the following motley picture:

Native Peoples in the Police Zone, 1932

Bushmen	4,370
Hottentots	17,762
Bastards and Coloured	8,746
Damara	24,691
Herero	24,276
Ovambo	6,333
Others	2,868
Total	89,046

Some of these ethnic groups have presented problems altogether out of proportion to their numerical strength. One outstanding example was that of the Bondelzwarts, a Hottentot tribe with some European admixture, who had revolted once before in German days. They went into laager in 1922 and had to be subdued by force of arms. A hundred of the tribesmen were killed, and the official enquiry which followed brought to light the distrust which survived from earlier days between Black and White in the country, as well as the discontent of a people driven to exasperation by grievances which they probably exaggerated, but for which they could obtain no redress. Not a little seems to have been due to the lack of experienced officials, familiar with the ways of these particular Natives. (13) The Permanent Mandates Commission, in reporting on the matter, expressed its regret that the obvious difficulties of the situation should have 'justified, in a territory under mandate, the treatment of the Natives as indicated by the evidence'. (14)

A further difficulty arose with the Rehoboth Bastards, a small group of Coloured people who had enjoyed a wide measure of autonomy during the German occupation. The Union authorities endeavoured to define these rights in consultation with the Kapitein, or Headman, and members of the Raad, or Council, of the Rehoboth Gebiet. Under an Agreement made in 1923, a measure of local self-government was recognized, and the Raad became one of the organs of administration in the Gebiet. This solution was opposed by many of the Bastards and, in consequence, the powers of the Raad were temporarily vested in a Magistrate. There followed a brief episode of resistance which the Mandatory suppressed by force of arms in April, 1925. When order was restored, a majority of the Rehoboths still refused to recognize the Agreement of 1923, and, relying apparently on a promise alleged to have been made by General Botha in 1915, claimed independence for the Gebiet. The Union Government appointed a Commissioner to report on the constitutional position and other cognate matters, but there was considerable delay, and the Rehoboths twice forwarded petitions to the League of Nations in 1926. The tension has, however, been relieved, excitements have cooled down, and the Gebiet has relapsed once more into its curious, if somewhat unexciting, normal self.

These incidents have been outlined on account of the publicity they received, rather than by reason of their intrinsic importance. In many ways, indeed, the chief interest of the post-war period is to be found not in the limited happenings within the Police Zone, but rather in the gradual extension of administration over the tribes of the North and East. A few officers of the Native Affairs Department went out into these remote areas soon after the War, established friendly contact with the local Chiefs, and used their influence to promote recruiting for the mines. Europeans required special permits to visit Ovamboland, the Okavango and the Kaoko-veld, and, at first, missionaries were only allowed to go there provided they gave a written undertaking to encourage the recruiting of Native labour. (15) In course of time this onerous condition was with-drawn, and the recruiting of labour throughout South West Africa is now carried out by the mines themselves, with the assistance of an official ap-pointed by the Administration.

The whole of Ovamboland was declared to be a Native Reserve in 1929. At the same time Trust Funds were set up for the principal Ovambo tribes. These receive the proceeds of an annual levy of 5s. from each adult male, which the tribesmen had been induced to pay voluntarily. The money is expended after consultation with the Chiefs or Headmen. (16) Tribal organization is much more developed in Ovamboland than elsewhere in the territory. Of the eight Ovambo tribes, four are ruled by hereditary Chiefs, and the others by Headmen selected by the people. In one of these areas, the somewhat unusual expedient was adopted for a time of appointing an administrative officer to act as Chief, but the normal rôle of the European Commissioner is that of an adviser to the Chiefs and Headmen. He has his own Native agents in all the tribes, and endeavours, by periodic visits, to settle intertribal disputes, and to keep in touch with local opinion. (17) Ovamboland would seem to offer a promising field for administration through existing tribal agencies, and might provide an interesting example of 'indirect rule' under Union auspices.

This possibility was unfortunately not in the minds of the framers of the Native Administration Proclamation of 1928 which, in the main, followed fairly closely the general principles of the Union Native Administration Act of 1927, though, unlike its prototype, it made no provision for conferring judicial powers upon Native Chiefs. In general, the Administrator was given power to appoint or remove Chiefs and Headmen; to prescribe their duties and privileges; and to exercise all authority recognized as belonging to any supreme or Paramount Chief by Native Law and Custom. A Chief Native Commissioner is the principal officer, under the Administrator, for all Native affairs, and Native Commissioners and Assistant Native Commissioners may be appointed for any area where large numbers of Natives reside. They may be given criminal jurisdiction over any offence committed by a Native, which is concurrent with that of the Magistrate of the district, if any: and civil jurisdiction in matters concerning Natives only, with certain specified exceptions. They are empowered to administer Native Law and Custom, provided it is not opposed to principles of public policy or natural justice. (18)

The Proclamation was put into force in 1930, but does not seem as yet to have made much difference in administrative practice. Apart from one or two urban areas, jurisdiction over Natives within the Police Zone is still exercised by Magistrates, though the Native Affairs Department is responsible for administration outside.

The Mandatory is pledged not only to administer the territory but also to promote to the utmost the material and moral well-being and the social progress of its inhabitants. This is not an easy task in a poor country like South West Africa, unless one adopts the facile view that work for a European master is the finest education for the Black Man. Indeed, one of the Administrators of the territory once declared to the Permanent Mandates Commission 'that the best way of bringing civilizing influences to bear on the Native was to remove him from his own environment and place him in a European environment'. (19) Such, however, is not the declared policy of Government in educational matters. 'The aim is definitely not to Europeanize the Natives. They must retain their language and customs as far as the latter do not clash with the great general principles on which civilization rests'. (20)

In South West Africa, as elsewhere, Native education is in the hands of the Missions, the Administration paying for teachers' salaries and for supplies of furniture and equipment in approved schools. A conference of educationalists and missionaries, held in 1923, decided upon the policy of training selected men of each race as teachers. The difficulty hitherto has been to find suitable persons from each of the many peoples of the land, and to obtain adequate financial support.

The expenditure officially described as being incurred on behalf of Natives is summarized in the following table.

Expenditure on Natives (21)

	(£ thousands)	
	Average for the 5 Years 1927–8 to 1931–2	Provision for 1932–3
Education	12·2	13·1
Native Affairs	22·5	12·7
Public Health	9·1	9·4
Irrigation	4·0	—
Public Works	0·4	—
Total	48·2	35·2

During the five-year period, expenditure on Natives thus averaged some £48,000 a year, or under 6·4 per cent. of the total ordinary expenditure of the territory, which amounted to £756,000 a year during the same period. When all allowances are made for the costly nature of administration in a country both large and poor, and for the further fact that the principal Native taxes which, however, only bring in some £7000 a year, are earmarked for the Reserves, the share of total expenditure accruing for Native services can hardly be described as high. Under such conditions, development must needs be very slow, though this is probably inevitable in any case in a country where the population averages well under one to the square mile.

The Mandate system implies a certain minimum of principles which are often easier to define in the abstract than in the concrete. It is not concerned, as such, with any particular theory of administration, direct or indirect; but, inherent in the doctrine of trusteeship, is a view of Native policy very different from the crude doctrine of exploitation which characterized the government of South West Africa in earlier days. The transition to this newer and more humane outlook must, of course, take time; but the doctrine itself stands as a challenge not only to the Administration of one vast and arid territory, but also to the framers of Native policy in other parts of Africa.

NOTES AND SOURCES

In the following Notes, reference will be made to the various publications and documents which have proved most immediately useful. It will suffice here to indicate a few of the works which are of more general interest, even if they are referred to later.

On the bibliographical side, mention must be made of the *Subject Catalogue of the Library of the Royal Empire Society, formerly Royal Colonial Institute*, by Evans Lewin, M.B.E., Librarian, vol. i: *The British Empire generally and Africa* (1930).

A survey of most of Southern Africa will be found in vol. i of Professor R. L. Buell's massive work: *The Native Problem in Africa*, published in 1928.

On the historical side, a good general introduction is Walker, E. A., *A History of South Africa* (1928). A most useful book on the Native question is Brookes, Edgar H., *The History of Native Policy in South Africa from* 1830 *to the Present Day* (2nd ed., 1927), though, unfortunately, the absence of an Index is a very serious handicap.

For the organization and functioning of the Native Affairs Department in the Union, Rogers, Howard, *Native Administration in the Union of South Africa being a brief survey of the organisation, functions and activities of the Department of Native Affairs of the Union of South Africa* (1933), is indispensable. It is a comprehensive survey, from a departmental point of view, to which it is a pleasure to express one's obvious indebtedness.

Amongst recent official publications, special mention should be made of the *Report of Native Economic Commission*, 1930–2 (U.G. 22, 1932).

An interesting study of many problems, Native and other, will be found in *Complex South Africa: An Economic Footnote to History* (1930), by Professor W. M. Macmillan.

For present conditions in Swaziland and Bechuanaland, the official reports of Sir A. W. Pim (Cmd. 4114 and 4368) are essential.

I. *The Union of South Africa*

1. Governor Sir George Grey to the Right Hon. Sir George Grey, Bart., Dec. 22nd, 1854 (q. Brookes, Edgar H., *The History of Native Policy in South Africa from 1830 to the Present Day* (2nd ed., Pretoria, 1927), p. 91).

2. Cape Native Blue Book, 1882, p. 6 (q. Brookes, *op. cit.* p. 254).

3. The 'Glen Grey' Act, No. 25 of 1894 (Cape of Good Hope).

4. Letter from the Prime Minister's Office to the Chief Magistrate of Tembuland and Transkei of Sept. 21st, 1894 (q. Kenyon, J. T., *An Address Delivered at the University of Stellenbosch on the General Council Administrative System of the Transkeian Territories* (1932), p. 30).

5. Kenyon, *op. cit.* p. 35.

6. Brookes, *op. cit.* pp. 52–3.

7. Royal Letters Patent of April 27th, 1864.

8. Pretoria Convention of 1881, art. 21 and 22.

9. Brookes, *op. cit.* p. 128.

10. Transvaal Law, No. 4 of 1885, art. 2.

11. The Native franchise in the Cape, although exercised by so few people, has come to be regarded as something almost sacrosanct by progressive Abantu in the Union. Its retention they somehow consider as a guarantee of equality of treatment in the future. In fact, it is already very much a thing of the past. The Women's Enfranchisement Act of 1930 introduced the principle of adult female suffrage for Europeans throughout the Union. Act No. 41 of 1931 introduced universal adult male suffrage for Europeans in the Cape, though Natives and Coloured can, of course, still qualify under the property and literacy conditions of earlier legislation. This is, however, made difficult in practice. In 1929 there were 15,780 Natives on the electoral roll in the Cape; in 1931 the number had fallen to 12,271. (See *The South African Outlook* of December 1st, 1933: Article by Linton, A., 'The Native and Coloured Franchise'.)

12. Memorandum by S. O. Samuelson, Under-Secretary, of September 1907 (q. Brookes, *op. cit.* p. 74).

13. Native Affairs Act, No. 23 of 1920, sec. 2.

14. *Ibid.* sec. 16.

15. *Report of the Native Affairs Commission for the year 1921* (U.G. 15, 1922), p. 52.

16. By the Natal Act, No. 1 of 1909, the Colony was divided into four districts, each under a District Native Commissioner. These 'districts' comprised several magisterial divisions. The scheme proved unworkable, and was drastically amended by Union Act No. 1 of 1912.

17. Chief Native Commissioners have been appointed as follows: (i) for the Transkeian Territories, with headquarters at Umtata; (ii) for Natal and Zululand, at Pietermaritzburg; (iii) for the Ciskeian Districts, at King William's Town; (iv) for the Witwatersrand Districts, at Johannesburg—this Official being also Director of Native Labour for the Union; (v) for the rest of the Transvaal and for that part of the Cape Province known as British Bechuanaland. This latter appointment is held by the Under-Secretary for Native Affairs *ex officio*.

18. Native Administration Act, No. 38 of 1927, sec. 2, as amended by sec. 3 of Act No. 9 of 1929. A number of magisterial districts, especially in Zululand, have been handed over to the Department of Native Affairs, which counts amongst its officials 47 out of 149 Native Commissioners, together with 8 out of the 9 Additional Native Commissioners, and 46 out of the 58 Assistant District Commissioners hitherto appointed under the Act. (Position in 1933: *vide* Rogers, Howard, *Native Administration in the Union of South Africa*, p. 14.)

19. The following statement of eighty years ago is interesting in this connection: 'Looking at the importance of the Kaffir Department, and bearing in mind that if it goes wrong all goes wrong, the Commissioners are of opinion, that that is the Department of the public service which should take the precedence of all others, and must be rendered efficient at any cost; that every other branch of the Service must be curtailed to the utmost, rather than

158 NOTES AND SOURCES

that the Kaffir Department should want in efficiency from the lack of pecuniary support'.

Thus the Natal Native Affairs Commission of 1852–3; *Report*, p. 58 (q. Brookes, *op. cit.* p. 171).

20. Native Administration Act, No. 38 of 1927, secs. 25 and 26.

21. A list of important Proclamations (1928–33) is given in Rogers, *op. cit.* p. 26 sq.

22. Cf. Walker, E. A., *A History of South Africa* (1928), pp. 580–1.

23. For area and population see *Year Book of the Union of South Africa*; and for the Reserves, Rogers, *op. cit.* p. 119. Morgen are here converted into acres at 1 Morgen =2⅓ acres.

24. Tsewu v. *Registrar of Deeds* (1905 T.S.C. 130).

25. For these estimates and details of the whole question see Rogers, *op. cit.* pp. 148–51.

26. For a recent discussion of this system see *Report of Native Economic Commission*, 1930–2 (U.G. 22, 1932), pp. 51–8 and 185 sq.

27. Cape Province: Private Locations Act, No. 32 of 1909. A Private Location is there defined as 'any number of huts or other dwellings on any private property occupied by one or more Native male adults who are not servants'.

28. Transvaal Law No. 21 of 1895. The word '*bywoner*' (or *bijwoner*) is frequently used as a generic term for the whole of the landless class, and is often regarded as synonymous with 'Poor White'. A bywoner is, strictly, a customary tenant who enjoys no legal protection for his holding and whose status is approximately that of a squatter. He is often a poor relation of his landlord. On the whole question see Macmillan, W. M., *Complex South Africa*, pp. 87–103.

29. Natal Ordinance to prevent unlicensed squatting and to regulate the occupation of land by Natives, No. 2 of 1855. *Orange Free State Law Book*, chap. xxxiv, amended by Law No. 4 of 1895.

30. *Report of the South African Native Affairs Commission,* 1903–5, para. 193. For the recommendation *re* squatting see para. 181.

31. Thompson and Stilwell *versus* Kama (A.D. 1917, p. 209), where it was held that the effect of sec. 8 (2) of the Natives Land Act, No. 27 of 1913, was to exempt the Cape Province from the operation of the restrictive provisions contained in sec. 1 of the Act.

32. As to the Free State, see Natives Land Act, No. 27 of 1913, sec. 7: and for the transition in the Transvaal and Natal, sec. 6 (c). The definition of the term 'farm labourer' is given in full in sec. 10.

33. *Ibid.* sec. 6 (a).

34. Under the South Africa Act a two-thirds majority of a joint sitting of the Senate and the House of Assembly is necessary to change the Cape Native Franchise. (9 Edward VII, c. 9, sec. 35 (1).)

35. The following table shows the approximate areas involved:

Province	Million acres		
	Native Reserves	Scheduled Areas, Act No. 27 of 1913	Released Areas, Natives Land (Amendment) Bill
Cape	12·7	12·9	3·2
Natal	6·3	6·3	0·6
Transvaal	1·9	2·6	10·3
Free State	0·2	0·2	0·2
Total	21·1	22·0	14·3

See Rogers, *op. cit.* pp. 119 and 171. Morgen converted into acres at 1 Morgen $=2\frac{1}{6}$ acres.

The *Report of the Natives Land Commission,* issued in 1916, vol. I (U.G. 19, 1916), contains a great number of statistical data, though the area figures for the Reserves are somewhat higher than those given above. The following is a summary of the estimates of area and population made by the Commission (see *Report*, pp. 3–5):

Union of South Africa

	In thousands	
	Area in Morgen	Native Population
Reserves	11,164·5	1,929·6
Mission Reserves	538·3	94·6
Native-owned land	1,002·0	123·6
Crown Lands occupied by Natives	942·3	121·1
European-owned lands:		
(1) occupied by Europeans or unoccupied	105,712·3	1,286·3
(2) occupied by Natives	4,156·3	325·2
Total Rural Population		3,880·4
Total Urban Population		537·2

36. Native Labour Regulation Act, No. 15 of 1911. In respect of compensation see also Miners' Phthisis Acts Consolidation Act, No. 35 of 1925.

37. By the Natives Advances Regulation Act, No. 18 of 1921.

38. The recruiting of labour for the mines now takes place in increasing measure in the Union itself, and the Witwatersrand has come to depend much less on outside sources of supply. In Republican days arrangements were made for recruiting workers in Portuguese East Africa, though after the Boer War recourse was had to Chinese labour. In 1909 a Convention was concluded between the Transvaal Government and the Portuguese authorities which was finally superseded by a fresh Convention signed in 1928. This was to be operative for a period of ten years, unless a revision of its terms were called for by either Government after five years—a provision of which the Union Government availed itself in 1933. The Convention provided for a progressive reduction in the number of Natives of Portuguese East Africa who might be recruited for work in the mines to a maximum of 80,000 by the end of the first five-year period: limited the duration of service

contracts: and made provision for the institution of compulsory deferred pay. In actual fact, the number of Portuguese Natives has fallen well below the maximum agreed upon and very marked changes have taken place in the geographical origin of Natives employed in the mines, as may be seen from the following figures:

Natives employed in Labour Districts* (thousands)

Origin	At End of Year					
	1910	1921	1922	1928	1931	1933
Union	168·3	151·8	173·9	190·8	227·0	273·5
Basutoland	10·8	24·1	20·8	23·7	35·2	39·7
Bechuanaland	2·3	3·3	4·2	3·6	4·8	7·0
Swaziland	4·3	5·0	6·8	5·6	6·7	7·1
H. C. Territories	17·4	32·4	31·8	32·9	46·7	53·8
Portuguese East Africa	100·8	90·9	86·4	105·7	73·4	55·7
Other	6·7	3·2	3·7	5·2	5·9	6·7
Total	293·2	278·4	296·0	334·7	352·9	389·7

* Prior to 1922 Transvaal only: Proclaimed Labour Districts (including Kimberley, etc.) thereafter.

Of course the large increase in the number of recruits from the Union and from Basutoland and the Protectorates of recent years has been stimulated by the long period of drought and its concomitant of acute agricultural depression. With better conditions in the rural areas, it is improbable that the local labour supply will be so abundant as it was in 1933.

39. Natives (Urban Areas) Act, No. 21 of 1923, sec. 5, as amended by sec. 3 of the Natives (Urban Areas) Act, 1923, Amendment Act No. 25 of 1930.

40. *Report of the Native Economic Commission*, 1930–2, para. 722.

162   NOTES AND SOURCES

41. *Report of the Native Economic Commission*, 1930–2, para. 728. Two of the members of the Commission advocated the complete abolition of the Pass System (*ibid.* para. 741 and Addendum by Mr Lucas, paras. 358–60).

42. Native Administration Act, No. 38 of 1927, sec. 28.

43. Under authority of sec. 19 of Act No. 25 of 1930.

44. Natives (Urban Areas) Act, No. 21 of 1923, sec. 28.

45. Natives Taxation and Development Act, No. 41 of 1925. The local tax is imposed in respect of every hut or dwelling in a 'Native location'. This term is defined in sec. 19. Exemption is granted to indigent Natives; to any Native, whose permanent home is outside the Union, who produces proof that he has paid the current taxes in his permanent home; and also to any Native in regular attendance at an approved educational institution (sec. 4 (1)).

46. South Africa Act, 1909 (9 Edward VII, c. 9), sec. 85 (iii), where this was done 'for a period of five years and thereafter until Parliament otherwise provides'. No action has as yet been taken in the matter by the Union Parliament.

47. These are the official figures for the purposes of Act No. 5 of 1922. Actually the Cape Province and the Transvaal erroneously excluded from their calculation the sums of £16,000 and £5000 respectively, which they continue to contribute themselves.

48. Financial Relations Fourth Extension Act, No. 5 of 1922, secs. 9 and 10.

49. This was enacted, not by the Natives Taxation and Development Act, but by the Provincial Subsidies and Taxation Powers (Amendment) Act, No. 46 of 1925, sec. 3. It has been mentioned here for the sake of convenience.

50. Act No. 41 of 1925, sec. 13, as amended by Act No. 37 of 1931, sec. 8, and Act No. 25 of 1932, sec. 9.

51. The figures summarized in these three paragraphs are given in full in Rogers, *op. cit.* p. 104.

52. *Report of the Native Economic Commission*, 1930–2, paras. 1064–7.

53. *Ibid.* para. 1058.

54. *Ibid.* especially paras. 207 and 212, for the expression of similar views.

55. Native Administration Act, No. 38 of 1927, secs. 12 and 20, as amended by sec. 6 of Act 9 of 1929.

56. *Natal Code of Native Law*, Proclamation No. 168 of 1932, sec. 18.

57. For the early history of exemption in Natal see Brookes, *op. cit.* pp. 58–9.

58. This was effected by the Native Registered Voters Relief Act, No. 39 of 1887, usually known as the 'Hofmeyr' Act.

59. Native Administration Act, No. 38 of 1927, sec. 31, as amended by Act No. 9 of 1929, sec. 8.

60. Cf. *Report of the Native Affairs Commission for the year* 1921 (U.G. 15, 1922), p. 30.

61. See United Transkeian Territories General Council: *Proceedings*, etc., at the Session of 1933, pp. xcvi, xcvii, lxxx and lxxix.

62. See Proclamation No. 191 of 1932, chap. IV.

63. *Ibid.* para. 21 (a) and (b).

64. Native Affairs Act, No. 23 of 1920, sec. 5.

65. Native Affairs Act, 1920, Amendment Act, No. 27 of 1926.

66. For list see Rogers, *op. cit.* pp. 83–4.

67. It is not possible to enlarge on the general question of Native Education in the Union, which has been excellently summarized by Dr E. G. Malherbe in *The Year Book of Education*, 1933 (Editor: Lord Eustace Percy), pp. 601–24. The spread of secondary education of recent years must, however, be mentioned, nor can one omit a reference to the South African Native College at Fort Hare. In close proximity to Lovedale, that classic home of Native Education founded by Scottish Presbyterians nearly a century ago, the S.A. Native College aspires to University rank. It was established in 1916, and later incorporated under the Higher Education Act of 1923. A number of its students, who include a few Coloured and Asiatics, have already taken external degrees of the University of South Africa. The importance of the College will be greatly enhanced by the recent decision to institute a course for the training of members of a new Native medical service, more especially for work in the Reserves.

68. This problem has recently been submitted to a very thorough-going analysis by the Carnegie Commission. Its report was published in five volumes under the title: *The Poor White Problem in South Africa* (Stellenbosch, 1932). Unfortunately the preliminary summary in vol. i, called 'Joint Findings and Recommendations', is very brief, while the body of the work is, inevitably, somewhat long. The Commission regard the problem itself as denoting 'principally the economic and social retrogression of a considerable part of the White rural (or originally rural) population' (vol. i, p. v). They suggest, as a conservative estimate of the number of very poor, 300,000 in 1929–30, though not all of them were 'Poor White' in the technical sense (vol. i, p. vii). They note that 'the economic and social decline here discussed is particularly noticeable among the White population of older settlement' (vol. i, p. viii), and believe that the principal cause is to be found in 'mal-adjustment to modern economic conditions'. Their principal recommendations are for increased educational facilities and a better organization of welfare work. This Report is a contribution of great importance to all interested in South African conditions or in inter-racial contacts.

69. They describe this as 'a race against time'. See their *Report*, para. 103.

70. The Mines and Works Act, 1911, Amendment Act, No. 25 of 1926, gave power to restrict the grant of certificates of competency in specified occupations, and in such areas as might be named in the regulations, to Europeans, Cape Coloured and Mauritius Creoles or St Helena persons.

71. Cf. the view of Mr J. H. Oldham: 'Segregation may not, indeed cannot, be the ultimate ideal. But at a particular stage in the development of the human race, it may be the arrangement which, on the whole, makes most for harmony and peaceful progress (*Christianity and the Race Problem* (1924), p. 170).'

II. *The High Commission Territories*

1. Section 151 of the South Africa Act of 1909 (9 Edward VII, c. 9) reads as follows: 'The King, with the advice of the Privy Council, may, on addresses from the Houses of Parliament of the Union, transfer to the Union the government of any territories, other than the territories administered by the British South Africa Company, belonging to or under the protection of His

Majesty, and inhabited wholly or in part by Natives, and upon such transfer the Governor-General-in-Council may undertake the government of such territory upon the terms and conditions embodied in the schedule to this Act'. This schedule establishes the principle of legislation by proclamation, and stipulates that the advice of a Commission of at least three members, holding office for a period of ten years, shall be taken in administrative matters. A Resident Commissioner is to be appointed for each territory, for which separate annual estimates shall be prepared. The several budgets are to be credited with the duties on all goods imported into the territory, and all revenue shall be expended on behalf of the territory itself, subject to a contribution towards the cost of defence and other common services of the Union proportionately not greater than the relation borne by the Customs revenue of the territory to the total Customs receipts of the Union. The inhabitants of the territories shall be entitled to move freely throughout the Union, subject to any Pass regulations in force; and no land shall be alienated in Basutoland or in the Native Reserves of Bechuanaland and Swaziland. If any or all of these territories were in fact transferred, the Schedule could, presumably, be amended or repealed by the Union Parliament under the powers conferred by sec. 152 of the Act.

2. The Customs Agreement of June 29th, 1910 terminated the Customs Union Convention hitherto in force and brought the independent administration of Customs to an end in the three territories. Each of these was to receive an equitable share of the duties collected. This was based on the average proportion of the total received during the three preceding financial years.

3. Proclamation of March 12th, 1868. See *Basutoland: Orders in Council, High Commissioner's Proclamations and Government Notices*, issued during the period from March 12th, 1868 to June 30th, 1913 (1913), p. 12.

4. Order in Council of February 2nd, 1884. Proclaimed on March 18th, 1884. *Ibid*. pp. 1–2.

5. Regulation No. 4. *Ibid*. p. 14.

6. See *The (Amended) Basutoland Native Laws of Lerotholi* (printed as a pamphlet), Law 4.

7. Proclamation of March 31st, 1910. See *Basutoland: Orders in Council, etc.*, p. 121.

8. See, for example: Hodgson, M. L. and Ballinger, W. G., *Indirect Rule in Southern Africa* (No. 1), *Basutoland* (1931). The authors do not appear to be familiar with the working of 'Indirect Rule' in other parts of Africa, and are strongly opposed to tribalism as such. Many of their specific criticisms thus lose somewhat in persuasiveness. They also pay what seems to be inadequate attention to the achievements of the administration in education and public health. In this pamphlet, as in the much more interesting study they have published on Bechuanaland, their solution of the economic problem is apparently that there should be a great increase in the burden already borne by the British taxpayer on behalf of the three Territories.

9. See *Report of the Native Economic Commission*, 1930–2, Part VI, pp. 160 and 165–8.

10. The *Report* (made by Sir A. W. Pim) *on the Financial and Economic Position of the Bechuanaland Protectorate*, 1933 (Cmd. 4368), is an indispensable guide to present-day conditions in the territory.

11. The quotations in this paragraph are taken from a letter, describing the interview, and later approved by the Chiefs, which was sent by the Colonial Office to the Rev. W. C. Willoughby. It will be found in C. 7962 (1896), *Correspondence relative to the visit to this country of the Chiefs Khama, Sebele and Bathoen and the future of the Bechuanaland Protectorate*, pp. 21–3.

12. See *Bechuanaland Protectorate: Orders in Council and Proclamations:* June 30th, 1890 to December 31st, 1929 (1930), pp. 141–4, for text of Proclamation No. 9 of 1899, which defined the boundaries of the Bamangwato, Batawana, Bakhatla, Bakwena and Bangwaketse Reserves.

13. By Order in Council of January 10th, 1910. *Ibid*. p. 13.

14. See Note 2 above.

15. Proclamation No. 9 of 1909. See *Bechuanaland: Orders in Council, etc.*, p. 200.

16. Proclamation No. 47 of 1919. *Ibid*. p. 327.

17. Proclamations Nos. 1 and 16 of 1932, and High Commissioner's Notice No. 82 of 1933.

18. See Cmd. 4368 (1933), especially App. xxv: Effect of the outbreak of Foot-and-Mouth Disease on proposals for Development (pp. 193–4).

19. Order in Council of May 9th, 1891. See *Bechuanaland: Orders in Council, etc.*, p. 7.

20. Proclamation of June 10th, 1891. *Ibid.* p. 76.

21. Proclamation No. 2 of 1896: *ibid.* p. 115; and No. 40 of 1912: *ibid.* p. 247 sq.

22. Proclamation of June 10th, 1891, as amended by Proclamation No. 17 of 1922: *ibid.* pp. 349–50.

23. Proclamation No. 1 of 1919. *Ibid.* pp. 320–1.

24. Proclamation No. 19 of 1926. *Ibid.* pp. 450–1.

25. This point is made by Hodgson, H. L. and Ballinger, W. G., *Britain in Southern Africa* (No. 2), *Bechuanaland Protectorate*, p. 31.

26. At the time of going to press the Native Administration Proclamation, 1934, and the Native Tribunals Proclamation, 1934, only exist in Draft form, though it is anticipated that they will be issued during the course of the year. The former regulates the appointment, powers and functions of Native Chiefs, and gives legal recognition to the *Kgotla*, or customary meeting of the tribe. The latter distinguishes between Senior and Junior Native Tribunals, regulates the disposal of fines, and insists upon the keeping of records of all cases heard.

27. For the Convention of 1894 (art. II) see Hertslet, Sir E., *The Map of Africa by Treaty*, I, 256.

28. See *Swaziland: Report for* 1907–8 (Cd. 4448–5: 1908), p. 13.

29. See Proclamation No. 28 of 1907. *Swaziland: Orders in Council, Proclamations and Principal Government Notices*, from June 25th, 1903 to June 30th, 1908 (1908).

30. See *Report* (by Sir A. W. Pim) *on the Financial and Economic Situation of Swaziland*, 1932 (Cmd. 4114), p. 18. Like the later Report on Bechuanaland, this gives an authoritative account of conditions in the Protectorates.

31. Proclamation No. 2 of 1915.

32. For these figures see *Report* (by Sir A. W. Pim) cit., pp. 6–7 (Morgen have been converted into acres in the ratio of $1 : 2\frac{1}{9}$) and p. 22.

33. Sobhuza II and Miller, *Law Reports*, A.C. 1926, p. 518.

34. Proclamation No. 4 of 1907, art. 17. *Swaziland: Orders in Council, etc.*, p. 49.

35. For a summary of the economic resources of the country see *Report* (by Sir A. W. Pim) cit., esp. p. 7 sq.

36. *Ibid.* p. 14.

37. Proclamation No. 10 of 1906. *Swaziland: Orders in Council, etc.*, p. 42.

38. For the growing dependance upon the mines, see note 38 in Section I above (p. 161).

39. See *Report* (by Sir A. W. Pim) cit., pp. 25–6.

III. *Southern Rhodesia*

1. For a summary of British expansion north of the Limpopo see Evans, Ifor L., *The British in Tropical Africa* (1929), chaps. XII and XIII.

2. Charter of Incorporation of October 29th, 1889, sec. XIV.

3. On the causes of the rebellion of 1896 see *Report* (by Sir R. E. R. Martin, K.C.M.G.) *on the Native administration of the British South Africa Company, together with a letter from the Company commenting upon that Report*, July 1897, C. 8547, esp. pp. 6, 39 and 44.

4. Southern Rhodesia Order in Council of October 20th, 1898. This revoked the Matabeleland Order in Council of July 18th, 1894, while preserving many of its stipulations.

5. *Ibid.* sec. 12.

6. *Ibid.* sec. 79; and for details of the organization of the Native Department see Regulations issued by the Chartered Company for the good government of Natives, 1898 (text in Hone, P. F., *Southern Rhodesia* (1909), pp. 51–8).

7. Ordinance No. 21 of 1904. Strictly speaking the tax as fixed in 1901 (Ord. No. 12) was still called a Hut Tax, though it was made payable in respect of every adult occupant of a hut,

8. Southern Rhodesia Native Regulations Proclamation, No. 55 of 1910, secs. 13 and 14.

9. Cf. Hone, P. F., *op. cit.* p. 59: 'The decay of the personal and moral authority of the indunas is doubtless another safeguard against rebellion'.

10. Cf. *Report of the Native Affairs Committee of Enquiry*, 1910–11 (Salisbury, 1911), p. 6.

11. *Ibid.* p. 5 sq.

12. Hone, P. F., *op. cit.* p. 59.

13. *Report of the Native Affairs Committee of Enquiry*, 1910–11 (1911), cit., p. 2.

14. Southern Rhodesia Order in Council of 1898, sec. 81.

15. Resolution of Executive Council of October 27th, 1902 (Mashonaland), and November 5th, 1902 (Matabeleland).

16. See *Papers relating to the Southern Rhodesia Native Reserves Commission*, 1915 (1917: Cd. 8674). The Native Affairs Committee of Enquiry, 1910–11, expressed the view that the Reserves were adequate in area for the present needs of the Natives and for the reasonable expansion of the population in the future, but considered that the delimitation of some of the Reserves was inconvenient, and that finality should be achieved by legislation. (See *Report*, cit., p. 11.)

17. *Papers, etc.* (Cd. 8674), pp. 11–12.

18. Southern Rhodesia Native Regulations Proclamation, No. 55 of 1910, secs. 8, 9 and 12.

19. Proclamation No. 32 of 1913.

20. Southern Rhodesia Order in Council, 1898, sec. 80. In point of fact, this section was taken over, with a slight change in the form of drafting, from the Matabeleland Order in Council of 1894.

21. Southern Rhodesia Order in Council, 1898, sec. 83, reads as follows: 'A Native may acquire, hold, encumber and dispose of land on the same conditions as a person who is not a Native, but no contract for encumbering or alienating land the property of a Native shall be valid unless the contract is made in the presence of a Magistrate, is attested by him, and bears a certificate signed by him stating that the consideration for the contract is fair and reasonable, and that he has satisfied himself that the Native understands the transaction'.

22. Under Letters Patent, of 1st September 1923, providing for the constitution of Responsible Government in the Colony of Southern Rhodesia.

23. *Ibid.* sec. 26 (2).

24. *Ibid.* sec. 28 (a).

25. Under Letters Patent, of 1st September 1923, providing for the constitution of Responsible Government in the Colony of Southern Rhodesia, sec. 39.

26. *Ibid.* sec. 42.

27. *Ibid.* sec. 43. Cf. Note 21, above.

28. See *Report of the Land Commission*, 1925 (C.S.R. 3, 1926).

29. *Ibid.* esp. paras. 49, 121, 122, 132 and 134.

30. *Report of the Native Affairs Committee of Enquiry*, 1910–11, p. 9.

31. Private Locations Ordinance, No. 14 of 1908, promulgated 3rd June, 1910.

32. *Report of the Land Commission*, 1925, cit., para. 356.

33. *Ibid.* para. 369.

34. Land Apportionment Act, No. 30 of 1930, secs. 21–8.

35. *Ibid.* secs. 6–11 and sec. 3.

36. *Ibid.* secs. 15–16.

37. *Ibid.* secs. 18–20.

38. The figures are taken from the *Reports* of the Chief Native Commissioner for 1924, 1928 and 1932 respectively. In the case of the last named year, the small separate entry for the Fingo location is excluded from the total.

39. This was the opinion of the Land Commission of 1925. See their *Report*, cit., para. 66.

40. Land Apportionment Act, No. 30 of 1930, secs. 29–33.

41. E.g. in the *Report* of the Chief Native Commissioner for 1930 we read: 'In general the Chiefs have functioned satisfactorily. It is growing yearly more apparent, that with a few notable exceptions, they are slowly losing the little influence which remains to them' (p. 14).

42. Native Affairs Act, No. 14 of 1927, as amended by the Native Affairs Amendment Act, No. 8 of 1931.

43. Criminal Trials (High Court) Act, No. 18 of 1927, sec. 4.

44. Letters Patent of 1923, sec. 47.

45. *Report of the Commission appointed to enquire into the matter of Native Education in all its bearings in the Colony of Southern Rhodesia*, C.R.S. 20—1925.

46. Native Development Act, No. 5 of 1929, sec. 1.

47. See *Report of the Director of Native Development for* 1929, p. 61.

48. The visit of the Phelps-Stokes Commission to East Africa in 1924 enabled the local governments to learn something of the methods adopted in the U.S.A. for dealing with backward Negro communities in the rural areas. In the following year the Government of Kenya founded the 'Jeanes School' at Kabete, near Nairobi, which also received some financial assistance from the Carnegie Corporation though not from the Jeanes Fund. Its primary object is to train visiting Native teachers and their wives (village guides) for social and educational work in the Reserves. Similar institutions now exist in Nyasaland and in Northern Rhodesia.

49. Figures for Southern Rhodesia from *The Official Year Book,* 1932, pp. 459 and 470. The figure of expenditure on Native Education in the Union is the amount paid to the Provinces for that purpose, together with the share of expenditure on Union Education allocated to Natives by the Native Economic Commission. (See their *Report,* paras. 599 and 1100.)

50. Cf. *Report on Industrial Relations in Southern Rhodesia,* by Professor Henry Clay (C.S.R. 3, 1930), esp. paras. 122 and 123.

51. At the time of going to press a change in policy seems to be foreshadowed in Southern Rhodesia. This will apparently include the imposition of a local tax in the Reserves, the proceeds of which will be supplemented by a £ for £ grant from the Government, and earmarked for development expenditure in the Reserves.

IV. *South West Africa*

1. Let not the reader think that this is written in a spirit of mere chauvinist invective. The words are quoted from a standard German work, *Das Deutsche Kolonialreich,* ed. Hans Meyer, 1910, vol. II, p. 290. The genial author there writes of the Bushmen in the following words: 'Mit solchen Menschen können Kolonisten nicht rechnen: man lässt sie leben, solange sie wenigstens keinen Schaden anrichten. Wo sie diese Forderung aber nicht erfüllten, hat man sie wie Raubwild abgeschossen'.

2. For an outline of the administration see *Deutsches Kolonial-Lexicon* (1920), esp. articles on 'Deutsch Süd-West Afrika', 'Eingeborenenrecht' and 'Eingeborenensteuern'.

3. *Report of the Administrator of South West Africa* for 1922, p. 11.

4. See the evidence given by Major Herbst (on the question of the Bondelzwarts Rising of 1922) before the Permanent Mandates Commission in 1924. League Publication: A. 19, 1923, VI, esp. pp. 120 and 129.

5. 'The Native question which, in South-West Africa, is synonymous with the labour question, is one of considerable difficulty for which the Natives are least of all to blame.' (*Report* of the Administrator for 1920, p. 13.)

6. Union Act No. 42 of 1925, sec. 26 (a).

7. *Ibid.* sec. 7 (i).

8. The European population of South West Africa was 19,432 at the Census of 1921; 24,115 at that of 1926; and was estimated at 32,840 in 1931.

9. Native Administration Proclamation, No. 11 of 1922, sec. 16.

10. *Report of the Government of the Union of South Africa on South-West Africa* for 1928, p. 57. (These Reports will henceforth be referred to as '*Report* to the League'.)

11. Proclamation No. 9 of 1924.

12. Natives (Urban Areas) Proclamation, No. 34 of 1924.

13. See on the whole question: *Report* of the Commission appointed by the Government of the Union of South Africa to enquire into the Rebellion of the Bondelzwarts (U.G. 16, 1923).

14. *Report on the Bondelzwarts Rebellion* of August 14th 1923 submitted by the Permanent Mandates Commission to the Council of the League of Nations. (L. of N., A. 47, 1923, VI, p. 5.)

15. See *Report* to the League for 1925, pp. 107–8.

16. Ovamboland Affairs Proclamation, No. 27 of 1929. A Trust Fund was instituted in the Caprivi Zipfel in 1930.

17. See *Minutes of the Permanent Mandates Commission*, League of Nations Publications, C. 568, M. 179, 1928, VI, pp. 84–5, and C. 305, M. 105, 1929, VI, p. 63.

18. Native Administration Proclamation, No. 15 of 1928.

19. See *Minutes of the Permanent Mandates Committee*: League of Nations Publications, C. 405, M. 144, 1926, VI, p. 39.

20. *Report* to the League for 1930, p. 51.

21. These figures are summarized from the more detailed revenue returns for the individual years given in the *Report* to the League for 1932, p. 18.

INDEX

(a) *Principal Statutes, Orders in Council and Proclamations*

(*b*) *General Index*

NOTE

The map shows the approximate distribution of Native areas South of the Zambezi, except in Swaziland, where it would be difficult to indicate their limits on so small a scale. Particular thanks are due to the South African Institute of Race Relations for permission to incorporate data from an outline map of the Union: and to the Mandates Section of the Secretariat of the League of Nations for similar assistance with regard to South West Africa.

This map of Native areas should, of course, be compared with others showing rainfall, physical features and population density, which are more easily available.

The numbers in the map refer to the following areas:

Union

1. Glen Grey
2. Fingoland
3. Tembuland
4. Pondoland
5. Zululand
6. British Bechuanaland

H. C. Territories

7. Basutoland
8. Bamangwato Res.
9. Bakwena Res.
10. Bangwaketse Res.
11. Batawana Res.
12. Bakhatla Res.

S. W. Africa

13. Rehoboth Gebiet
14. Bondelzwarts country
15. Ovamboland

In South West Africa the shaded portions represent the Native leases and the Treaty Reserves as they existed in German days, including the Rehoboth Gebiet. The additional Reserves, including Ovamboland, created under the administration of the Mandatory are shown in black. Elsewhere all the Native areas are in black. In the case of Southern Rhodesia, the Native Reserves alone are indicated.

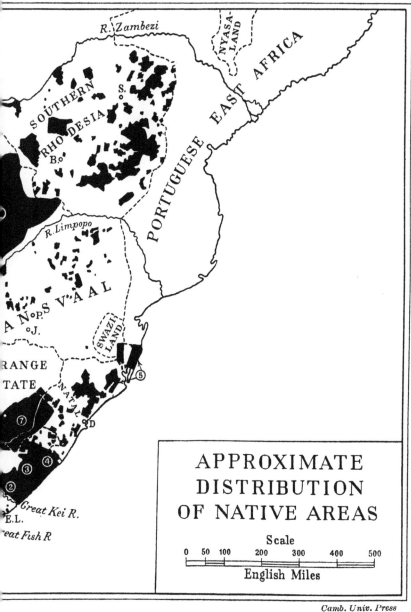

R. Zambezi

NYASA-
LAND

SOUTHERN

S.
o

RHODESIA

B.o

PORTUGUESE EAST AFRICA

R. Limpopo

A N.o P. S V'A A L

o J.

SWAZI-
LAND

ORANGE
STATE

NATAL

⑤

⑦

o D

③ ④

②

Great Kei R.

E.L.

Great Fish R

APPROXIMATE
DISTRIBUTION
OF NATIVE AREAS

Scale

0 50 100   200   300   400   500

English Miles

Camb. Univ. Press

For EU product safety concerns, contact us at Calle de José Abascal, 56–1°,
28003 Madrid, Spain or eugpsr@cambridge.org.

www.ingramcontent.com/pod-product-compliance
Ingram Content Group UK Ltd.
Pitfield, Milton Keynes, MK11 3LW, UK
UKHW012331130625
459647UK00009B/221